GW00394021

KIND YET FIRM:
DISCIPLINE YOUR TODDLER THE POSITIVE PARENTING WAY

Develop Your Child's Respectful
Behavior with Love & Limits, Eliminate
Tantrums and Establish a No-Drama
Environment in Your Home

GRACE STOCKHOLM

TABLE OF CONTENTS

GAMES AND ACTIVITIES FOR POSITIVE DISCIPLINE

Here's what you'll learn from this bonus:

- My top 7 games and activities to teach your child about discipline the positive parenting way
- How to craft the tools for the games at home
- Why it is so important to teach your kids to play and learn at the same time

Toddler discipline, and well, life in general, is much easier when everyone in the house is having some fun!

Get your 7 games and activities right here:

http://gracestockholm.net/toddler-discipline-fun-games/

INTRODUCTION

We, as parents, wish to see our children becoming the model kids of our society. We want to see them laughing, smiling, happy and playing while being best at whatever they choose to do and displaying exemplary character along the way. No wonder it's a dream of every parent, seeing how far-fetched the very idea seems! But is it, even some of it, achievable? There is no doubt that parenting is no easy matter. There are hurdles and difficulties every step of the way. Though each stage in a child's life presents varying challenges for a parent, the most challenging for a parent are often the toddler and the teen ages. The challenges of parenting a toddler are many. From power struggles to tantrums, handling meltdowns to dealing with bad behaviors, parents have to brave it all. It's little wonder, then, that most parents feel a deep sense of frustration and depression engulfing them when anything and everything they try with their kids seems to be a failure. Parents begin to question their own worth and abilities as parents. What is going wrong? Why doesn't the child listen when instructed? How do we teach kids discipline? How do we teach them to behave while around company? These and many more questions plague a toddler's parents constantly. Is there a solution to this? There definitely is.

It is important as a parent to understand your child's emotional as well as physical needs. Several problems amongst toddlers stem from the fact that parents are unable to understand what key element is missing from their development. Issues also arise when parents are not clear as to their own roles with respect to their kids. A child needs to have a loving and stable parental presence at all times. Along with love and stability, give your child definite discipline strategies that have been researched and painstakingly developed for the very reason of providing your child the right balance of firmness and nourishment that they need. Understanding your child's behavior and providing healthy alternatives is just as essential.

There are some amazingly effective strategies developed for addressing the parenting concerns of parents around the world, such as the most effective positive parenting discipline program developed by Jane Nelson. There is also the very inspiring and effective conscious parenting developed by Dr. Becky Bailey. These and many more such programs are designed based on the parenting philosophies developed after tireless work done by Alfred Adler and Rudolf Dreikurs. There are several approaches to parenting, but only such positive parenting techniques bring forth your desired results. Adopting a positive parenting way to deal with your children ensures you have stronger parent-child relationships. Kids will have better and higher self-esteem. You will be able to enjoy better communication with your kids. When the atmosphere at home is peaceful and happy, you will also see a marked difference in how your child performs at school, in social situations, and other activities. With this book, I aim to bring you the core essence of the inspiring works of these great experts.

By reading and employing the strategies enumerated in this book, you will be able to form a calm and respectful relationship with your child. You will be able not just to control and handle tantrums and bad behavior, but you will also be able to understand why your child is acting the way they are. You will be able not just to calm your child in stressful situations and handle bad behavior effectively by providing healthy alternatives, but you will also be able to calm yourself and take care of your own mind and body in such stressful situations. It is essential that parents take care of themselves too amidst all the stress and frustrations of handling tantrums and constant power battles with kids. Using this book as a guide, you will be able to confidently nurture an understanding and respectful relationship between yourself and your child, just the way you've dreamt it.

Parenting isn't easy. It is even harder when you have little toddlers with their own minds to deal with. From tantrums, stubborn behaviors, emotional meltdowns, to unpredictable mood swings, your toddlers are sure to give you a taste of every possible experience. What you need at this juncture is a way to be a peaceful and confident parent who doesn't resort to yelling, spanking, or being harsh in any way. This book will help you become that parent.

CHAPTER 1:

DISCIPLINING YOUR TODDLER THE POSITIVE PARENTING WAY

Before we begin our foray into the world of parenting, let us take a moment to analyze ourselves and see what it is that we wish to achieve through our parenting.

What is the intention behind it? How do we approach the whole parenting concept? With what attitude? This is necessary on so many levels. It is good that parents nowadays are looking for positive changes to make to the system of parenting so that our children do not suffer or face the issues we did when we were kids. And yet, it so happens that our traditional methods of parenting are so ingrained in us that we unknowingly fall back to the way our parents treated us. Therefore, if we can take a moment to pause and reflect on our attitudes toward parenting, it will set the right mindset for us before we begin.

Now, our approaches can be of three kinds. One, which is the forceful or punishing attitude, where when you see your child misbehaving, your immediate reaction is to stop it and you use force to do so, often punishing your child, many times harshly. This can cause resentment to build within a young mind over time. The second approach is to be entirely too permissive, where you rescue your child from every conflict situation. You replace their problems with solutions that you have thought for them. This, again, is hindering the child from growing and developing their personality. The third kind of attitude would be to mold, teach, and encourage your child to learn from their mistakes, solve problems on their own, and it involves being empathetic. Your intention as the parent is the key here. What or how would you want your child to be when they grow up? Keep that bigger picture, that bigger goal, in your mind always.

We shall begin by understanding the various forms of parenting that are prevalent in our society. At one extreme, we see parents that are too strict, uninvolved, and non-inclusive of their children's needs and wishes. These are authoritarian parents for whom their decision is final and their say is to be followed at all times at all costs. At another extreme, we have extremely lenient parents for whom kids dictate matters in every sphere and they simply go with what their children wish for. This is permissive parenting and can be no better than the over-strict parent, for even this parenting style adds little to a child's personality. Then we have the non-caring, non-responsive parents for whom nothing their child does ever matters and they do not bother themselves with parenting issues and kids. This is, by far, the worst style of parenting, for this is neglectful of children and brings the very health, growth, and existence of the child into question.

But, there is one style of parenting that is inclusive, responsive, and attentive to the needs and wishes of the children. This is the authoritative style of parenting. It is where parents are empathetic toward the feelings and needs of the children, along with being firm and tough whenever and wherever necessary. This is the style that gives you the best results in terms of personality development in a child, for this method involves the right balance of nourishing love and firmness.

But even within an authoritative style to get the maximum benefit, one must use the style the right way. Many well-meaning parents who wish to implement this style, and be understanding of their children's needs and, at the same time, set firm limits, stumble when it comes to 'how' to do it. How does one decide what is the right amount of firmness? What reaction is appropriate for a child to be called empathetic enough? Where do we draw the line between showing empathy and being firm? Is listening to what children say and agreeing with them called being empathetic? These and many more such questions trouble parents from time to time. This is where positive parenting comes in, and this is where this book comes in.

Understanding Traditional Method of Discipline

Traditionally, we see parents resorting to force of some kind to get their point across and to get their kids to obey them. Yelling, calling names, and belittling a child's abilities are common enough occurrences in a household that practices the traditional style of parenting. It is important to acknowledge that even these parents love and show concern for their kids. But at times that demand a softer, positive, and understanding approach, they lose the control of their own emotions and frustrations which get transferred onto the child in the form of punishments, eventually taking a toll on the parent-child relationship.

Consider this as an example. Your son is refusing to eat dinner and insists he is given the ice cream he saw you put in the freezer a while earlier. He begins to cry and thrash around at the table, and eventually even attempts to take the ice cream from the freezer himself, stomping his feet the whole time. What do you do? Initially, you try to tell him how he cannot have ice cream before dinner and that you will give it to him only after he finishes his food. But when he ignores you, you proceed to threaten him with punishments, or perhaps a 'no-dessert-for-three-days' rule. This is what will mostly occur in the traditional style of parenting. After the initial attempt at calming the child, parents turn to punishments and threats to bring the situation under control.

This is not beneficial for so many reasons. It is just as though you are saying, "Do as I say, not as I do!" One must understand that at the end of it all, your child is just that, a child. They are young and innocent and need loving care and empathy. Their reasoning is not mature enough to understand why you would deny them that ice cream. For them, it is a simple enough wish, easy to fulfill for you, and yet they are threatened with punishments. It is hard for them to understand why. This can eventually lead to the child building a wall of resentment toward the parent that the parent might find difficult to break down with all the love and care they have to offer, if at the next turn of bad behavior this resentment is only strengthened with the threats they still offer.

How Does Positive Parenting Differ?

In a positive parenting atmosphere, your reaction would be different. What you focus on here is presenting to the child a reasoning that they can understand with ease. You wish your son to wait until dinner is finished before eating ice cream. For this, you do not simply insist he obey you, but you rather give your reasoning for it. This might not necessarily mean giving the child the complex reasons behind an adult's decision, as can be the case in a different scenario, but to make things understandable at his level. In our example, the parent can say something like, "I understand you want to have ice cream, and I want to have ice cream too. But, you know, I wanted to eat with you. That would be a good way to enjoy it, don't you think? So, let's finish this dinner quickly and we can both enjoy nice big scoops of ice cream together!" The key here is to get down to the level of the child and talk to them in a way that lets them understand your perspective too.

Positive parenting is child-centered. The focus here is on being responsive to the child's emotional needs and understanding the cause behind the child's behavior and responding to that causative reason. This is more in the lines of saying, "Do as I do."

Positive Parenting and Toddler Years

Toddler years are the time when a child begins to think on their own and have a mind and opinion of their own. This is a new experience to them and understandably is not something they can control consciously. As said earlier, their minds are still developing, and their reasoning is too immature in these years to fully comprehend why certain actions are inadvisable or why certain others are necessary. Keeping this delicate point in your mind while dealing with kids of this age is just as important.

Positive parenting isn't easy and will take time to get used to. It is indeed time-consuming and patience-demanding on the part of the parent. Yelling and getting it over with would be a lot easier. But, when you have all that you can achieve through positive parenting laid out before you, it is simply worth it to take that fortifying deep breath and walk the bridge. You need an agreeable and understanding mind and this is more so for toddlers. But because the toddlers are still young, moldable and malleable to a large degree, it is easier, and also extremely important, to implement the positive parenting approach for this age group.

As time-consuming as it is, it is important to instill the right attitude early on through positive parenting. The earlier you begin, the better it will be for your child in the long run. And needless to say, the benefits of positive parenting far outweigh the troubles a parent has to go through in implementing it. A little more patience is a tiny sacrifice in the bigger picture of your child's shining personality development.

CHAPTER 2:

AGE APPROPRIATE TODDLER BEHAVIOR

One of the first steps to take toward a successful parenting experience is to understand why a toddler behaves like a toddler. When we have fully understood the underlying reason for their ever-changing moods and wishes, then we can take whatever necessary steps are required to ensure a healthy relationship between you and your child.

Why Do They Do That?

From one to three years of age, a child is changing drastically. From being utterly dependent on you for their every need, nourishment to clothing and what not as an infant, to gradually being able to have a mind and say of their own in things, is an entirely new experience for them. As a child begins to walk and explore, they are introduced to the many colorful facets of the world around them that are suddenly at their disposal. Adding to that, they are now able to talk! How liberating might that be! They are able to voice their opinions and thoughts on various subjects. They are able to vocalize their likes and dislikes with confidence now, and this is a massive achievement for them.

At this stage, developmentally, a child is self-centered and focuses on their own needs and wishes. They are curious and inquisitive to an extreme. Based on the Piaget developmental theory, toddlers are unable to think outside their own lived experiences. They are now able to talk, yet their language is not fully developed to be able to communicate their moods and desires effectively. Largely, this is also because a child doesn't truly understand their own reasons for certain behaviors. Like for example, a boy who is hungry might not understand that it is hunger that is troubling him. He might cry for chocolate, throw things around, trouble his sister and so on. All this because of hunger and being unable to understand their own needs and put their feelings into words. This is what potentially leads them to tantrums.

At the core of their development, a toddler still very much needs a loving and caring touch. Being responsive to a toddler's needs in the moment is the key. Their brains being still in the process of development, toddlers lack a fully developed prefrontal cortex. This is where all the reasoning stems from. No wonder, then, that toddlers find it difficult to comprehend when an adult tries to reason with them at an adult level.

Developmental Milestones

Children develop certain specific skills as they continue to grow and age. These specific skills are known as developmental milestones. Though each child develops differently, there are a few basic milestones that most kids are supposed to cross at a certain age. We will see a few of these developmental milestones for each year in the toddler period.

One Year

At 12 to 24 months, most kids will be able to perform certain physical and sensory functions such as:

- Stand without support.
- Walk either unaided or with one-handed support.
- Participate in pretend play, like pretending to eat with a spoon, or speak on a mobile, etc.
- Can say a few words. Mostly call mother and father with their names, like mama or dada etc.
- Is able to point at objects with their pointer fingers.
- Is able to wave goodbye.
- Is able to participate in simple ball games, like throwing a ball back and forth.
- Is able to follow simple one-step instructions, like, "Give me the ball."

Two Years

At two years old, your child will be able to more or less perform the following functions.

- Is able to run.
- Stand on tiptoes.
- Climb stairs unaided, or with one-handed support.
- Is able to kick and throw a ball with ease.
- Solve simple puzzles.
- Is able to follow two-step instructions like, "Pick up the book and place it on the table."
- Imitate and play with other kids.
- Is able to go through a book, one page at a time.

From the age of one year to two years, there is a considerable change in your child. You will notice that your child is speaking more words now and is beginning to voice their likes and dislikes. This is also primarily the age when tantrums begin. This is the time when they begin to wish for things to go their way. But, at the same time, they are extremely malleable, can be easily diverted, and their thoughts easily molded. This, of course, is a huge plus, for you would want to make use of this age to deter them from tantrum-like behaviors or huge emotional meltdowns and teach your child, and yourself, how to cope with these situations.

Three Years

At three years of age, your child would have crossed quite a few milestones. By now, they will be able to do a few of the following actions with ease.

- Is able to identify familiar colors.
- Is able to fantasize with more imagination.
- Can follow three-step instructions.
- Is able to understand and remember time periods, like, morning, afternoon and night.
- Is able to count objects to some extent.
- Is able to sort objects by shapes and colors.

At three years of age, your child is considerably more mature. They are more involved in their plays and activities. They have more developed language and communication skills. Their social skills are better and they are relatively more confident. Though they still experience a little separation anxiety when faced with being separated from their parent or their familiar surroundings, they are now a little more sure of their place and standing.

Developmentally, toddlers lack what is known as emotional and impulse regulation. In our brains, emotions are mostly handled by a small almond-shaped cluster of neurons in the region called the amygdala. This develops slowly and is relative to the slow emotional development in toddlers. This is the reason why a simple craving for a piece of cake can lead them to cry uncontrollably while thrashing on the ground, leaving us dumbstruck and wondering why they can't understand that there's no cake in the fridge at present. Now we know why they cry or get upset easily. Also, you will see that in children, the 'hijack of amygdala' is pretty common. When faced with stressful situations our brain generates what is known as the fight or flight response to combat the stressful situations. This is where breathing exercises to calm the brain are so helpful. We will see more about breathing exercises in later chapters.

The prefrontal cortex in our brain is responsible for handling impulse regulation. This is yet underdeveloped in a toddler and this is the reason why we see poor impulse control in them. Toddlers tend to be impulsive, acting in the spur of the moment and often throwing us off balance. Now that we know why those excessive meltdowns (lack of emotional control) or the sudden running about at the shopping mall (lack of impulse control) occur, we will be in a better position to handle and care for them. Toddlers are inherently built to be impulsive and reactive. It is we who need to tailor our parenting methods to their emotional and physical needs.

Disorders and Labels

Many parents and caregivers are frightened into believing that their child might be 'different.' All kids are not the same. Many have attention span issues, hyperactivity, aversion to sleep, an affinity for one kind of game only and so on. These are all 'normal.' Just because your child is not like your friend's or neighbor's kid in one skill or another, does not make them abnormal. Each child is precious and is unique in their own way. Each child has their own strengths. The more accepting and understanding parents are of this reality, the less stress they or their children will face in their lives. Nowadays, attaching medical-sounding labels to each and every uniqueness that a child can have has become the norm. And with no surprise at all, we see several of these labeled children going on to become phenomenal in their respective fields of choice with no hint of those labels in their adulthood whatsoever. Therefore, unless expressly mentioned by a doctor of having some very obvious disability, refrain from attaching labels of disorders or using drugs for your children. You wouldn't want these labels to turn into self-fulfilling prophecies for your children.

CHAPTER 3:

COMMUNICATING EFFECTIVELY WITH YOUR TODDLER

Being able to effectively communicate with your child means that you are able to understand their calls for different needs and responding to those calls with an appropriate response. Doing this begins right from the age of infancy. It is nothing new for a parent to recognize, acknowledge, and answer these calls right from the time of birth. Babies cry and whine along with giving any number of cues to a parent for their many needs, from hunger or sleep to discomfort or needing to be held. Most parents are adept at recognizing these signs and responding to them appropriately. Even before the child is able to talk, they try and communicate with the help of cues. Cues such as pointing to a certain object when they need something, a bottle of juice perhaps, or holding up their hands when they need to be held, are common with kids who are yet unable to talk. It is important that a parent or caregiver acknowledges these cues and responds accordingly.

Using Appropriate Nomenclature

It is important that parents and kids resort to using proper names for their day to day used objects. Making a habit of using proper names for items regularly used goes a long way in ensuring that your child learns them quickly, and this makes for swifter communications. Using correct names for everyday items encourages a child to learn them faster and use them correctly.

Avoid Baby Talk

The child might not yet know how to pronounce a certain word and might begin calling it by their own equivalent that might have a similar sound or a combination of similar sounding letters. For example, a child who wishes to say 'juice,' might instead say 'ja-ju'. This is fine, and while the child will learn to say juice over time, you can help them learn faster by saying 'juice' yourself and avoiding using 'ja-ju' for juice yourself. When parents use baby talk for different things to communicate with the child, it delays the learning curve of the child. Always try and use the proper names for objects and encourage your child to learn this way.

Respecting Your Child

Begin respecting your child early on. Even when they are young and unable to talk and communicate using words, make it a point to give them importance in interactions and include them whenever possible.

For example, if you are feeding your child, you could include your child in the activity by saying something like, "Would you like to hold this spoon while mommy feeds you?"

Or if you are giving your child a bath and you recite rhymes while doing so as a bath-time-play, you could ask your child what rhyme they wish for and you could both sing that together. The point here is to make the child feel valued, included and respected. We want them to understand and believe that their choices and opinions matter to us and we are ready to hear them out. It is essential that you begin to inculcate this feeling as early as you can. Being valued and validated goes a long way in incorporating confidence in kids from an early age.

Expressing Emotions

Kids being able to express their emotions efficiently is an important part of having effective communication. But to do this, they would need our loving guidance to show them what it is that they are feeling. A parent can help their child in this regard by helping them name the emotion they are feeling.

For example, if you notice your child sitting quietly after they have just waved goodbye to their grandparents, you could say something like, "I understand you must be sad because grandma left for her trip. Are you missing her already? It's ok to be sad."

Or something like, "You are pounding the table, you must be angry."

What this practice does is it gives a name to what they are going through or the feeling they are experiencing. This is extremely helpful when you would like to teach them how to react or behave when they experience a similar feeling again in the future.

For example, you wish to tell your child that they ought to look at positive or brighter things when they are sad. But to do this, they would have to know what being sad is in the first place. Like when their grandma has gone for the trip, you would want them to look at the brighter side of things with something like, "You can make a welcome back card for her when she comes back." Or when your child is angry, you might want to say, "Take a deep breath three times when you are angry." Only when your child is able to relate the name of the emotion to what they felt when they experienced it themselves will they be able to grasp and put your advice into practice.

Naming emotions is also essential when you want to teach your child what emotions are fine to express, and which should be controlled.

Positive Talk

Another important pillar to excellent communication with kids, especially in the toddler age, is to use positive talk. This is when what you say consists of what the child can, should or must do instead of what they can't, shouldn't, or mustn't do.

Avoiding Negatives

Make it a habit to talk to your child in positive sentences. When you know that what you are going to say will involve a negation or denial of some kind, use a positive alternative to it in its place. A straight out 'no' is more difficult for a toddler to process than a positive alternative. Consider the following dialog between a toddler and a parent.

Child: Can we go to the park today?

Parent: No, not today.

Child: Why not today? I want to go now! I am bored.

Parent: I told you not today. Go play with your toys now.

This scenario can quickly escalate into a tantrum or even a meltdown. Now see the same dialog without the negatives.

Child: Can we go to the park today?

Parent: I think we'll go to the park tomorrow.

Child: But I am bored now!

Parent: How about we both play with your toys now and we go to the park tomorrow?

You see that the child refrains from asking, "Why not today?" in the second scenario, because the parent hasn't really said, "Not today." Instead, they used a positive alternative. Also, it is important to notice that the parent has involved the child to validate their reasoning and choice of activity, along with offering to play with them themselves. It is an important approach to be mindful of.

Using 'no' frequently to answer your child's requests and wishes can turn them bitter from within. It generates a feeling of being denied time and again when faced with an outright no. Instead, if the same is relayed using a positive alternative, it doesn't have the same drastic effects and is more encouraging and confidence-building for the child.

Reframing

Also important is to avoid a constant barrage of negative instructions. If a child is used to hearing things like, 'don't do this, don't do that', on a regular basis, this can only sow resentment in the child's mind toward the parent. And that is not something a parent would ever want. See the following example to understand the scenario better.

If your child is running around in the house or jumping on the sofa, you are bound to say something like don't run and don't jump. Instead, you could simply reframe the sentences to avoid the negative and say something like, "We should walk inside the house. You may run when outside in the garden or the park," and "We jump on the ground and sit on the sofa."

You could even attach a line of caution with respect to values you follow at home or about their own safety that might be at stake due to their actions. But never begin your instruction or advice with a negative. Give up using 'don't' in such situations.

Doing this ensures your child doesn't feel restricted or denied simple pleasures constantly.

Practical Strategies for Effective Communication

There are a few actionable points that you can make use of and put into practice when you wish to communicate with your child with ease and efficiency. Keeping these tips in mind will help you talk in a manner that your child can easily understand and, at the same time, accept what you are saying for the value it carries. You will be able to reach your child more effectively this way.

Maintaining Eye Level

Always make it a point to talk to your kids when you are at their level. Get down, either on your knees or with your back bent, so you are on the same level with your child. Being on the same level as them is similar to taking them into confidence before saying anything. This simple step makes you more approachable and easy to understand. Even if what you are saying is not of an intimidating nature, your straight and unyielding stance can make it appear to be so. Therefore, it is always a good idea to talk to kids when at their same level. Also, when they are talking, and you are simply listening, being on their level shows interest on your part, and your child would, therefore, be more willing to talk and open up to you this way.

Affirm and Repeat

When your child is trying to tell you something, either through words, fully framed sentences, or just gestures and cues, it is always advisable to affirm their thoughts out loud. Repeat after them to let them know you are listening to them and are ready to hear them out and understand their needs or wishes. This is especially true in the case of younger kids of around two years who have just begun to talk. This can also help you understand them better when all you have are a few broken words or gestures to go on. Affirming their opinions and repeating after them gives them a chance to acknowledge if what you have understood is indeed what they have been trying to say or deny and alter their approach to help you understand better.

For example, "You are pointing at that teddy, do you wish to play?", or

"I understand you want to have ice cream but let's have it together after dinner."

Parental Narratives

Narratives are when you involve your child in your day to day activities by talking to them about the work you are doing, or telling them a story of your past or some hilarious anecdote from your childhood. The point here is to talk to them and make them feel involved. These simple narrations can help establish an atmosphere of ease around your child and help them be confident about opening up to you in a similar way when they need to. It also gives them a sense of importance to know that you think them important enough to share such things with them, and they will be more willing to reciprocate in the future.

For example, if you are making an omelet and your child is sitting at a table near you, just talk to them about what you are doing in a simple narrative. Or you could talk to them about an omelet related story from your childhood. Making them feel involved and valued is the key.

Being Present

Being available and approachable for your kids is a vital element in good communication with your children. When your kids are speaking to you, make it a point to give them your undivided attention and truly listen to what they wish to tell you. Take care to put away your phones, gadgets, books, or any other diverting items so that you are able to give your child your full attention when they are speaking to you. Respond to them with something that assures them that you have actually listened and are not taking them or their talk for granted.

Forming Connections Through Touch

Make it a habit to encourage connection forming rituals with your child. Let it be an activity that you perform with your child on a daily or regular basis that involves some form of touch. Giving a positive touch, like a hug, a kiss, or simply holding hands, is essential to make your child feel loved. And if you can make some form of it into a daily ritual, it will reinforce the idea of being loved in a child's mind. A simple loving caress, ruffling of hair, or a pat on the back are great tools to help the child feel loved and connected to you.

You could implement things like holding hands and praying before going to bed, or hugging and giving a kiss while waking up in the morning. These little rituals can go a long way toward making your child feel important and valued.

Name Calling

Many parents resort to name-calling and fixing undue labels on children. From as young an age as two years, children are termed as cry-babies, bed-wetters, trouble makers, messy birds, slow learners, black sheep, and more. These names are disrespectful to the child and nothing good can come from resorting to this practice. Not to mention, these names are unfair and hindering the development of your child. It is like telling them, this is what you do and this is what we expect from you. This can, in some cases, lead the child to grow resentful toward you for casting them in such a demeaning role. Or, they might grow rebellious, and instead of correcting their 'supposed' bad behavior that these names refer to, they will work toward establishing these names as true. In the end, it is your child's personality that will suffer, and indeed no parent would want that.

Many times, parents who understand and acknowledge that name-calling is wrong still resort to calling names unknowingly. How do we realize if we are doing this grave parenting error?

Stop and ask yourself if you, your family, relatives or friends have cast your child in a role that you haven't yet realized. Is your child comfortable with this name? Is it a negative or a positive name? Now, work toward negating the effects of this name-calling. Ensure everyone who comes in contact with your child is aware of how you do not encourage calling names. If you think the damage has already been done, and your little toddler has suffered from being called different names, still, it isn't too late. Look for opportunities to encourage your child positively for the very thing the name disrespects them. If a child is regularly called a crier, it might help to encourage them to counter the effects of this name when they haven't cried. If you are waiting at home for guests who are late, and your child is waiting along with you, without being whiny or impatient for eating the cake, they deserve something like, "You have been so patient. You haven't cried once. Good job!" The point here is to break the restricting chains that such name-calling throws around a child.

Avoid Promises

Whether it's you or your child who's making the promise, if it cannot be kept, then it is far better to avoid making the promise. Parents often tend to promise their kids things that they cannot do or take care of. If a child insists on going to the park, and you respond with, "We'll go tomorrow," when you are well aware that you have an important work meeting the next day is simply unfair. Such statements are common from parents who look to simply postpone or procrastinate a requested chore, even without paying any attention to this habit. It might be because you are tired, not well, just not in the mood, do not have the funds, or the time isn't right, that you look to put it out for a later time that is still impossible to achieve. These promises are like the tomorrow that never comes. Instead, when your child wishes something from you that you are not yet ready or able to give, simply say so. Toddlers are perceptive and intelligent, and if you tell them you are tired and not yet ready for it, they are more likely to understand you better than if you were to make an empty promise and not carry it through. Saying, "I am sorry. I am tired right now," is much better than "We'll play after one hour," and then finding you are still not ready after extending it by another hour.

We also see kids making promises to their parents. Make it a point to not take promises from them. "I don't take promises. Tell me when you are ready and we will talk then," is much better than taking them for their word and making them feel embarrassed or incompetent when they can't keep their end of the promise. It is better, therefore, that you abstain from taking promises from your children.

Promises are good when you are sure you or your child can keep the promise. Otherwise, it is simply a futile exercise to engage in empty promises with children as it breaks their confidence in you.

How Not to Talk With Your Child

As we learn how to talk with and address our children, it is wise to also be aware of what is it that we want to avoid. Because many of us have grown up hearing a lot of what is to follow, we tend to fall back on our parents' ways and repeat those same mistakes. We want our children to feel encouraged and motivated to be good when we talk to them instead of feeling put down and insulted. Let us see some of the ways in which a parent might speak and which are not uplifting for the child.

Commanding:
This is when the parent speaks in a commanding voice. This may sound like, "Come here at once," "Shut the TV off right now!"

Threatening:
This is when the parent is threatening the child to either do something and behave in some manner or face the consequences. "Stop jumping or you won't get to watch TV!" "Walk fast or I'll go without you!"

Blaming:
This is accusing or blaming the child for an action irrespective of whether they have committed the act or not. In both cases, it is still not empowering, neither you or your child, to talk so. "The thing is you don't listen." "Don't try to change the subject; I know you broke the glass."

Moral policing:
This is another unfair way of addressing your child. Comparisons with their siblings or their friends is never a good idea. Things like, "Look at your brother. He never gets in trouble." "Why can't you be like Amy, she is always so sweet!"

Sarcasm:
Talking with sarcasm is extremely insulting to a child. Imagine, would you want someone to talk sarcastically with you? How can a little

innocent child bear it when we adults cannot handle it ourselves? "You thought you could carry two full glasses at a time? Great idea! Look what you've done." "Wow, you spilled all the milk. What a great help that was!"

Dramatics:

Saying things like, "Stop shouting. My head is going to burst." "See what you've done! You've ruined my dress!"

Gaining Willful Cooperation

A few conversation points can be important and vastly helpful in gaining willful cooperation from your kids. You want them to cooperate with what you tell them. Keeping these little things in mind will ensure that your children cooperate with you. This is essentially for those kids who have already established a well-connected relationship with you. If you and your child share a special bond and have specific connection-creating practices in place (see chapter 6), then it most likely means your child is ready to cooperate with you and only needs little pushes from you to finally commit. If you are careful and aware of how you speak, then you can successfully achieve willing cooperation from your child.

Avoid the Accusatory 'You'

When you want your child to be proactive and cooperative, avoid the use of accusatory 'you' in your conversations. Instead of, "You spilled the milk," say, "The milk spilled. We'll need to clean this mess."

"You broke the vase," say instead, "The vase broke. Walk carefully or you might hurt yourself with the broken pieces."

Give a Little More Information or Explanation

Sometimes, children need a little more information or explanation with respect to what we are asking them to do. Of course, this might not always be possible, but whenever we can, it is good to at least explain a little of the reasoning behind our instruction, so the children feel valued enough to be shared such important knowledge. "When you place your glass back on the table with a lot of force, it can break. We need to be gentle." This is better than saying, "Be gentle. You'll break the glass."

"When you disturb Daddy while he is working, he can get angry." This is better than saying, "Don't disturb Daddy, or he'll punish you."

Accept Your Shortcomings

When you are not up to the mark on something, you aren't aware of what your child is asking about, you aren't feeling your usual healthy self, you are tired, or anything of this norm, it is better to share this with your child when they approach you with some expectations. This is better than avoiding or hiding things from them. This lets them understand that parents are not always perfect and they struggle just like they do. Parents have bad days just like them.

CHAPTER 4:

SETTING LIMITS AND GIVING HEALTHY CHOICES

Along with all the love that you can give to your child, your child also needs limits and boundaries set around them. These are for their own healthy growth and safety. It is important to realize that setting limits is just as essential for a child as giving them a hug.

Setting limits will help your child embrace good habits and make them empathetic toward others. There are a few key elements to keep in mind with respect to setting limits and being firm with your children. Let's look at these one by one.

Being Clear

One of the most important things to bear in mind is giving clarity to your child in all your instructions. Let your instructions, limits or boundaries be short and concise. Do not confuse the child with contradictory and complex instructions. Keep things simple.

For example, "We don't stand on the table. We sit on a chair and eat at the table." I have heard a parent include saying, "We don't stand on the table. But we can if we want to reach someplace higher. But you must not do that. That is only for elders."

The second part of the instruction was needless. It did nothing but add complexity to the set boundary. Toddlers are young, after all, and they do not need such complex instructions to confuse and baffle them. They would simply chuck all of it to the side and do what they want if the boundaries are too complex to even comprehend.

Therefore, make it a point to give clear, direct and simple instructions that the child can easily follow. You could make use of a picture chart or instruction chart of some kind to make things simple and easy for them to understand and stick to. Place such a chart in an area that they often frequent, like on the refrigerator door or the living place wall space, etc.

Types of Limits and Boundaries

Let us now understand what the different types of limits or rules are that must be in place for our toddlers.

Safety

Include in this bracket all the safety rules that you feel are necessary for your child to know. These would be what they can or cannot do in or around the house or even when out. Like, holding hands when crossing the street, waiting for you to head outside, not playing with hot or sharp things like scissors, needles, etc. Keep your rules short and to the point. Tell them why it is that you want them to follow these rules.

Behavior

These will form the bulk of your rules. Let them know what you expect from them in terms of good behavior. Again, keep your instructions short and avoid using negatives. Instead of saying, "Don't sit at the table to eat with dirty hands," try saying, "We wash our hands before we sit at the table to eat." It will also greatly help if you set an example for your child. Go with them to the bathroom and have both of you wash your hands before sitting at the table.

Include instructions on general day to day behavior, along with expectations for when in company, or when out of the house. One good way to ensure these limits are followed is to frame the rules in such a way that includes yourself in the limit too, wherever applicable. Like, "We answer softly and courteously when asked a question by a guest," or something similar. Using 'we' instead of 'you' makes it more acceptable and easier to acknowledge and apply for the kids. This helps avoid unnecessary power struggles between you and your child. Obviously, this is not always possible. When an instruction is specifically for them, make it a point to make it as inclusive, clear, and short as possible but retain the firmness of the instruction, without making it sound like a request.

Though it is good to practice courtesy with your kids in all your conversations, avoid excessive politeness when giving instructions and laying down rules. Do not say, "Please, don't jump on the sofa." Instead, say, "We sit on the sofa. We jump on the ground. Sit back down."

Being too polite with instructions can lead your child to take you for granted. You want them to learn politeness and courtesy but not at the cost of following your instructions. At all other times, be polite and engaging with your child but not at the time of setting down limits or issuing directives.

Time

One important point to teach your children is the value of time. Kids need to learn from an early age about managing time and working efficiently around set time limits. Learning time management early on can help your child immensely in the future. Habits like punctuality and good time managing skills can all become ingrained in your child when taught to value time from a young age.

Toddlers are too young to understand and take note of time as we do. When you tell them to finish a task in ten minutes, they don't really have an idea of how long that would be. Their idea of time is still underdeveloped. To counter this problem and still teach your child to value time, you can make use of a few helpful tips.

Use a timer, an alarm or some kind of stopwatch to time their various activities. If you are at the park and it's time to go home, you could tell your child they have a certain time limit left, say five more minutes, and set the timer accordingly. Use the timer to remind them when it is time to finally leave. For kids who are able to identify numbers, you could even point to a clock and direct them to watch the hands of the clock and finish a task by the time the hand reaches a certain number. This is an excellent way to teach kids to work by the clock and be mindful of time.

Values

These are limits that are related to your specific values as a family. What you follow and believe as important must be taught to the child from an early age. For example, if in your family, you always eat dinner together at the dinner table, then that is something to teach your child from an early age. Such value-filled boundaries can also be taught to your child to inculcate good habits from a young age.

Safe Areas

This is a very innovative and positively encouraging concept to provide a safe area in the house for your child. This safe area is supposed to be a place where your child can be themselves and be safe. Either a corner in a bedroom, a part of the outside porch or some such safely restricted area where the child is free to play as they wish and be safe at the same time. Let this place be where they can make a mess of things, where they can eat of their free will and just be without any restrictions, but within this safe area only.

To create such a safe spot for your child, take a few precautions to keep them safe from any kind of accident or injury. Avoid placing sharp objects or furniture with sharp edges in this area. Place plenty of cushions and soft rugs or carpets for them to jump on or roll about. Only place items in this area that can be spoiled or broken and still cause no hurt or heartache for either you or your child. If this area is outside of the house, like in the yard or on the porch, make sure to attach a baby gate and any other preventive locks needed to keep your child safe when in the area. If using furniture, make use of non-slip footholds or mats to avoid slipping and injury.

Though safe areas are meant to be entirely safe so the kids can play all alone and not accidentally harm themselves, for very young kids under two years, keep a caregiver or an attendee with them at all times, at least to monitor them from afar. Place all their toys and activity things at their level, so they do not climb other furniture to reach some place higher. Lock all doors and cupboards and keep all non-kid-friendly items away.

The basic idea of a safe area is to encourage your child to be themselves, to let them learn and explore by being free in a secure environment without restrictions and without fear of injuries. In a safe area, there mustn't be the constant need to monitor their every movement, to see that they don't fall, or don't touch something they shouldn't, or don't put things in their mouth that they mustn't. This is a great way to help your child be a little explorer in their very own corners.

Reasoning

It is always a good practice to explain your reasoning behind the various limits and rules to your child. Even if at first they are unable to understand or appreciate your logic, they will learn to acknowledge and accept your way of seeing things with time. If your child isn't supposed to go out alone, explain to your child as to why. Tell them how it isn't safe and they must wait for an adult to accompany them before venturing outside.

You would need to repeat your reasonings and your instructions again and again for a number of times. This would require patience and consistency on your part, but by keeping at it for a number of times, your child is bound to understand and accept your reasoning and follow accordingly.

Sticking By Your Limits

More important than simply setting limits is to stick by them. Kids are bound to resist and throw a fit when certain limits go against their wishes or what they would rather do, but it is your job as a parent to stick by what you have laid down.

Follow Through

You should always try to follow through with whatever you have instructed and planned out. You might have a rule of no phones, gadgets or screen time on weekdays, and if your child breaks the rule, you should have an idea of what the consequences are. Now, it is important that you stick to this rule and not let it become just a matter of empty words that are to be used to threaten and later forgotten with ease.

If your child breaks a rule, let them see the consequences of it. Keep in mind not to frame the consequences that are too harsh and which would ultimately be too difficult for you to follow through in the end. Let these be simple measures that you can carry out without remorse or regret. It is vital that your child sees you for the firm parent that you are, instead of being lenient when you have to actually put up a firm face to your instructions. This does not mean that you need to be harsh or demanding of your little ones, rather to be firm whenever you need to be.

At times you would need to intervene in your kid's activity to ensure your limits are met with. For example, if you are at the park and you tell your child that they have five more minutes to play and you begin the timer for five minutes. When the five minutes are up, you ask your child to come along, and instead, your child throws a fit and begins to cry. They may throw a tantrum or have a meltdown. At this point, you would need to intervene, maybe lift your child in your arms and walk out of the park, or sit beside them until they are able to relax. If you were to bend your will and extend the time by five more minutes, this could potentially go on forever or may even encourage your child to repeat such behavior in the future, too. Your love for your child would cause you to be lenient and giving in this matter, and this could negatively impact your child into taking advantage of your leniency in the future too. Instead, direct your love to be concerned of your child's future personality and character development. You want your child to respect certain boundaries set before them and respect the thoughts and feelings of people around them, too. This can only be achieved by being strong, firm yet loving in your limit setting, and making it a point to follow through with them when situations arise.

One good way to ensure follow through is to have pre-made agreements in place. When you involve your child in forming their limits and boundaries, they can even help you chalk out agreements to follow through when limits are crossed or expectations aren't met. For example, you can have a preformed agreement with your child that whenever they don't put their toys back in their place, they forgo playing with those very toys for a day. They may have it the next day when they assure you they will pick them up after playing. So, whenever they fail to pick up their toys after playing, you can simply remind them of your agreement with them and follow through with it. Such agreements are helpful in preparing the child as to what they can potentially face when they do not meet expectations or cross the limits.

Healthy Choices and Alternatives

It is important to give your children healthy options to what you have limited them from. They must be able to fall back on choices and alternatives that they can safely turn to when faced with a boundary. Toddlers are developmentally looking for areas to be independent in. They wish for autonomy both in their worlds and their bodies. This is one of the main reasons why toddlers throw tantrums when things do not go their way. As their sense of right and wrong is limited, it falls on the parent to present them with limits for things they mustn't cross and keep open for them options that they can easily be themselves with while exercising their freedom to choose.

Simple things like choosing the dress for the day, their choice of juice, or their option of a snack can help them feel validated and important. One thing to keep in mind is to always ask them by placing not more than two options before them and asking them to choose.

For example, do not put an open question like, "What would you like to drink today?"

Instead opt for something like, "Mommy has two juices, orange and grape, which one would you like?"

Doing this helps them exercise control over their choices and, at the same time, help them feel free to choose. It is simply a developmental milestone that they wish for a certain sense of freedom, and as parents, it is our job to honor that milestone by providing them with safe and healthy options that they feel free to choose from.

Keep in mind that all these choices are age-appropriate and do not present them with anything that is too adult or mature in nature. You don't want them to decide big things for you, or pick your next family vacation spot. You want them to feel free in accordance to their age with choices that are suitable to them.

Consequences Vs. Punishments

Many of us believe that consequences and punishments are interchangeable, and they are probably one and the same. It is not so. Punishments are when you make a child suffer and undergo some form of hardship when they make a mistake. They instill a certain amount of fear in the child's heart with respect to the mistakes they commit and also the adult punishing them. The focus of punishments is on what the child is not supposed to do, based on what or how an adult judges them as right or wrong. Punishments also cause the desire to please others, and getting in their good books becomes the motivation behind good behavior rather than the need to rectify based on reflection on one's mistakes.

Consequences, on the other hand, let your child understand and analyze where they were wrong. They encourage your child to take steps in order to correct them and prevent them from being repeated.

Consequences let your child undergo a learning experience and give them opportunities to improve themselves. The focus here is not on what the child is not supposed to do, rather what they can or must do to improve the situation and not repeat the same mistakes. Kids learn to own up to their mistakes and take responsibility for their actions.

Kids who are punished tend to enter into a state of denial and become defensive of their actions. It is also noteworthy to see how the same child gets punished over and over again for the same kind of mistakes. This is because punishment doesn't teach; rather it makes children stubborn and rebellious.

Now that we have understood the difference between consequences and punishments, let us understand what consequences look like and what are their various types.

Natural Consequences

These are what children face as a natural consequence of their actions. This is not you punishing them. Rather, it is them experiencing the natural consequence of their own actions and learning from it. What you do here is you let them experience the consequences instead of rescuing them. For example, if your child is banging a toy on the floor or jumping on the bed or sofa, what would be the natural consequence of these actions? In the first instance, the toy might break and your child might be hurt by any sharp edges of the broken toy. In the second instance, your child might slip and fall, and though the fall might not hurt much, it could be painful and might result in a few scrapes. If you start with "Don't do that, don't jump" etc., the child is most likely to ignore your admonishment and continue doing what they were doing. As a result, the toy might break or your child might fall. What would you do now? Many parents would respond with a "Didn't I tell you?!"

Instead, if you can start off initially not with a negative command but with a gentle reminder like, "Remember, we play with our toys in the proper way so that we are safe as well the toy is safe," or for the second scenario, "We sit or lie down on the bed or sofa." If, after this, your child goes on to ignore and continue with their actions and faces the consequence, instead of, "I told you so!" you respond with empathy and say something on the lines of, "You banged your toy truck on the floor and it broke. That's sad, but let's go see if we can fix it," or "that's sad, but let's put this in the trash and you can pick a different toy." For the second scenario, you would say something like, "You jumped on the bed and fell. That was painful. Let's go sit on the sofa and read a book."

The motive here is to help them over the hurt or sadness with empathy. The consequence is in itself enough to teach them that they mustn't repeat the mistake. The fact that you have let them experience the consequences without rescuing, blaming, or shaming is a good enough push for them to reflect on their actions and learn from them.

Natural consequences are useful when you can safely stand back and let your child continue so as to experience the natural results of their actions. Natural consequences must not be employed in situations when your interference is necessary, like situations where either your child or others could be seriously hurt. Natural consequences require you to act with respect and empathy, helping the child by providing support and a push toward reflection. By gently stating their actions that caused the result, you can nudge them into reflecting on their actions while being respectful and empathetic toward their suffering.

Logical Consequences

These are consequences that have been pre-arranged between you and your child. These types of consequences require you to be reasonable, empathetic, and respectful while offering consequences that are in some way related to the action committed.

For example, if your child is hitting other children, you could say something like, "Ben, you can either choose to continue hitting others and play alone as a result or you can stop right now and continue to play with everyone."

At this point, either Ben will stop hitting others and play normally or he might choose to ignore you and continue hitting. If he chooses to ignore, you can follow it up with something like, "You chose to continue hitting. It's hard, but you will have to play alone now."

Now the child might simply move to a different place to play alone, or he might respond with something hurtful for you. Do not, at this point, engage in a back and forth battle with the child. Do not respond with anger and encourage a power struggle. Instead, respond with empathy and say something like, "I know it's hard to play alone. I understand. But you can do it. Would you like to move to your quiet place to calm yourself first?" (Quiet place concept is covered in the later chapters). Once the child has calmed down, you can work to address the root cause of their hitting, but we first need to get the situation under control.

What the logical consequence does is introduce the child to what possible consequences might occur because of their actions. Try not to frame these as threats. Instead, say them as a matter of their own choice. Let the ball be in their court. What this does is allows them to reflect on their choices and actions, and if they face the consequence and you remain your calm and empathetic self, it forces them to pause and think about what they have done and how it has affected them and others around them.

It is important to frame logical consequences when the child is already connected to what you say and do. A child who feels unconnected will not respond to either of these types of consequences. When the child feels connected and loved, they will be more receptive to any type of consequence you present before them. Also, logical consequences must be related to the action or behavior of the child. Do not let your consequence turn into punishments by framing something that is entirely undoable, unreasonable, and unrelated to the behavior of the child. If the child is insisting on extended screen time and throwing a tantrum, you do not go ahead and say, "Either you comply and shut the phone or TV off now or you will have to forgo your supper." This is unreasonable and unrelated. This will not push the child toward reflection and understanding. The child would miss their supper and go to bed angry and resentful, along with being hungry. This does not teach the child anything.

Instead, you could say something along the lines of, "You have watched your thirty minutes of TV time. Now either you can switch off the TV and go play, or you will not get screen time next day/week."

Letting your child forgo screen time is doable both for you and your child in case they don't listen and do not shut off the TV. This also helps remind them that they are missing TV this week because they did not shut the TV off after half an hour last week. This is related to the action and hence will have more effect. Whatever your prearranged consequence will be, you want it to be something that you are able to follow through with it. And following through is important in order for the child to understand and reflect upon their actions and learn from them.

Understanding Obligations and Privileges

In many households, parents respond to misbehavior by taking away a few things from their children. This is done thinking that the removal of these things would set their children straight and teach them proper lessons. Though there is nothing fundamentally wrong with this concept, what needs to be clear is what it is that you are taking away. Parents have certain obligations upon them toward their children that they can in no way let their children go without.

These are the fundamental basic needs, both emotional and physical, that a parent has to fulfill for the child. These are things like healthy food, clothing, space to stay and rest, and respectful behavior. Taking away any of these basic necessities would be morally and ethically wrong, and it would amount to not fulfilling their obligations as parents.

There are other things, though, that are extras in the parenting equation. Things like special foods, extra lessons for the child, like guitar or music lessons, swimming lessons, or the like. These are privileges that a parent gives their children willingly. In cases of misbehavior or disrespect, if you feel that something needs to take a hit and get suspended for a while, it is these privileges and not the things under obligations. Under no circumstances should a child be asked to give up food or other basic necessities.

In the above logical consequences, we saw how a child was asked to play alone for a while, and how another child was asked to give up TV for the next weekend. These are privileges that are suspended for the time being and are bound to be much more effective than empty threats or harsh punishments.

It is important to note that when practicing positive parenting, we will aim to understand the cause underlying the child's behavior. While we do need to set limits and follow-through, it is essential, once the immediate conflict has been dealt with, to communicate with your child and understand where their behavior stems from. Only once we have been able to identify and take care of the real cause for the misbehavior, we can expect the circumstances to play out differently next time.

Practical Alternatives to Punishments

Now that we have understood how consequences are better than traditional punishments, let us now look at a few practical steps you can take in place of punishments.

Turning Anger Into Supportive Action

When your child misbehaves or acts in a way that angers you, stop for a moment. Your primary reaction is to perhaps shout or yell at your child. Instead of screaming your head off, you could instead channel your anger into supportive action for your child. You see your child trying to climb onto the counter to reach the cookie jar. What do you do? How do you react? In a non-positive usual situation, a parent would shout and scold their child. "What are you doing? You are not getting any cookies for a week now!" Instead, you could simply walk up to your child and put him down from the counter and say, "You want to get the cookies. Next time, tell me when you want one so I can help you."

Providing Choices Before Misbehavior

Earlier in the chapter, we saw how we must give children choices in place of the limits we have set for them. When they cross a boundary too, we present choices before them so they choose the right consequence. What we are seeing here is giving healthy choices to your children before they misbehave or are faced with a boundary. These are both healthy choices and they could choose any, so that either of those would prevent misbehavior and ultimately would prevent a consequence of any kind. For example, imagine the following.

You go to a shopping mall with your child. It's Christmas time and there is a huge rush. You go right into the mall without any preparatory talk, and when your child wriggles free of your grasp and runs about, you run around, shouting, "Come back this instant. You will have no screen time this weekend. Stop running."

Instead, if you could take a moment before getting into the mall and just talk to your child, saying, "There's a huge crowd in there. I'm afraid you could get lost. Either you sit in the car quietly with Grandma, or you come with me inside while holding my hand all the while. What do you choose?" Most likely this is going to work. If it doesn't, and your child still runs around, then perhaps a little talk and choices with logical consequence would be in order.

Let Children Make Amends

Many times it happens that a child forgets what they were supposed to do, or might have ignored your instructions for any reason. You see the job undone and you lose it. For toddlers, it could be simple things like picking up toys, putting back their books, helping sort clothes, etc. If they fall short of what you expected of them, do not shout and scold them for "not listening to you," for "always being troublesome," and so on. Instead, give them a chance to redeem themselves and make amends. Let them try and do the job they initially could not or did not do.

"The toys need to be picked up. Would you like to do it now?"

"There are dirty clothes on the floor. Pick them and put them in the basket."

Children are inherently innocent and pure. This gentle reminder is almost always enough for them to realize that they had initially forgotten or ignored doing the job, and you still aren't scolding them. This, in itself, is enough to push them into action. Toddlers being their young and innocent selves are most likely to be spurred into remedial actions because they would hate to have disappointed you. Seeing that

43

you are not angry or upset with them but are willing to work with them to give them another chance would be a great confidence boost for them and they will respect you more for it.

Using Consequence as a Teaching Tool

When a child misbehaves, we can let the consequence of it be an important teaching point. Consequences can be quite effective in teaching important lessons even without any explanations and lecturing on our part. Imagine, you take your child to the supermarket where they are constantly running around and pulling things off the aisle. What do you do? You come back home and could deny your child dessert after supper or reduce their screen time. But this wouldn't be a teaching point. Instead, if you can turn this into a situation that forces your child to think and reflect on their behavior, recognize where they went wrong and what they can do to correct it, that would be a true teaching point. If you are going to the supermarket again after a couple of days and you don't take your child along, they are bound to ask why they cannot accompany you. You respond, "You tell me, why can't you accompany me this time? Do you remember what happened last time?" This will encourage your child to remember and reflect on their behavior of the previous occasion, and they will understand that if they wish to come along, they will have to behave well.

This is a powerful way to instill valuable lessons in your child's mind. You don't yell, scold or deprive them of anything but rather turn your consequence into a teaching lesson.

Kind Yet Firm

One essential aspect that many parents forget is having the right balance of being kind and yet firm. Either the parent is exceptionally loving and kind, bordering on being too lenient and permissive, or the parent is too harsh and strict, bordering on being too controlling and authoritarian. Both of these approaches are not ideal. You do not want to be one and not the other; neither must you be kind at one time and be firm later on. Most parents are loving when the children are well behaved but turn into their strictest selves when they misbehave. This is not the most effective way to approach parenting.

What a child needs is you being kind and firm at the same time, in a single moment. Let your interactions be loving and compassionate while at the same time, you retain your own position of authority in the house and talk with firmness.

Observe the following sentences:

I know you want to keep playing with your legos, and your playtime is up. Either you put them away now, or I'll keep them in the garage. What would you like to do?

I know you are sad and want to have pizza right now, and we have pasta for dinner today. Would you like some more pasta sauce or cheese?

I know you don't want to go to bed now, and it's your bedtime. Would you like a princess story before you sleep?

These sentences show how a parent can stick to their limits while still being kind and understanding. They offer limited healthy choices and offer an understanding of the upset or sadness that setting limits results in. Parents are supposed to set boundaries, but this can be done with kindness too. Boundaries do not necessarily require you to be harsh. You must be firm and can also be kind at the same time.

Parents who are too lenient or too soft with their children need to understand that too much kindness is not always good for the kids. Read the following story of a little girl who, while playing in the garden, saw a cocoon of a butterfly upon a tree. The little girl observed that the butterfly was trying to get out of the cocoon. So she decided to help the butterfly along in its efforts by prying open the cocoon for it. As a result, the butterfly flew out of the cocoon but could not go far or high in the air, and after very little time in the air, it fell down and died. What do you think happened here?

The little girl with very good intentions of helping the butterfly, pried open the cocoon to facilitate its flight. But by doing so, she deprived the butterfly of the crucial muscle-building power which it acquires by struggling out of the cocoon on its own. On being eased out of the cocoon by the girl, the butterfly's flight muscles weren't developed. As a result, it couldn't fly high and died because of it. Too much kindness, in the end, killed the butterfly.

Parents who are too kind are often like that little girl. Even with the best intentions, they actually hamper the growth and development of their children by being too kind. Being too lenient, or rescuing too often, or not being firm with limits are all hampering for a child's development. This is why the right balance between being kind and firm is essential for the overall personality development of a child. Too much of any characteristic can have an adverse effect on how a child behaves.

CHAPTER 5:

ROUTINE AND CONSISTENCY

We have seen how important setting limits and following through on them is. Equally important is sticking to a schedule and being consistent.

Schedules give kids a sense of certainty. Following a fixed schedule is good for kids of every age. Right from the time of infancy a kid can be made to get used to routines and schedules. Having daily day to day activities organized and consistent at all times is essential to a child.

Routines

Routines are a predictable list of activities for the child. Through routines, kids are able to know what to expect throughout the day. Like for example, we sit at the table together as a family for dinner at night, we take a bath before bedtime, we read a book before going to sleep, we work in the garden after breakfast and so on.

These predictable activities help the child feel in control of their lives. When they know what is to come next, there will be fewer anxieties and fewer 'I am bored' troubles to handle for the parents.

Preparing For Transitions

When you and your child are faced with a situation that can alter your routines and upset your schedules, it is good to mentally prepare your child for this change beforehand. If the change is sudden and unexpected, you can do nothing about it, and you would simply have to wing it with your child. But when you are aware of an oncoming change in your life that can alter your schedules, it is advisable to ready your child accordingly.

For example, if you are headed to a vacation spot as a family, then this obviously would be a planned outing and is bound to alter your daily routines to a great extent. Giving your child a heads up as to what to expect would help ward off unnecessary meltdowns or unwanted anxieties on their part.

You could prepare your child maybe a week ahead by saying something like, "We are going to Disneyland, and it will be a lot of fun. We will stay in a hotel and things will be different. But, different could be a lot of fun!"

Repeat such reminders regularly till the time you make your move. This will help your child to be mentally ready for the coming change.

Need For Consistency

Routines must be consistent. If you have found a schedule that works for you and your toddler, then try and be consistent with it. Consistency is key in getting your child habituated to the schedules. If your chalked up routine or schedule has an activity which is skipped after following for a few days, then this will disturb the sense of certainty for the child.

This is true not just in terms of schedules and routines but with respect to your behavior too. When your child acts a certain way, you react in a certain manner. As a parent, you must keep your reactions consistent. If your child throws a tantrum, you must always respond in the same manner. If you let your emotions and frustrations rule your behavior at times, and respond with empathy at another time, then this would confuse your child and send out mixed messages to them. This is not advisable at all. Imagine if you see your child throwing a ball down the stairs and do not think much of it, so you either ignore it because it is an innocent game or because you are otherwise occupied and do not have the time or energy to spare a lecture for your child. In any case, you let it pass this time. Your child repeats the game the next day, when you are stressed about an entirely work-related problem. You respond by yelling and telling them off for being irresponsible and risking injury to others and to themselves. What do you think this does to your child? This is what sending out mixed signals means.

What can you do to avoid confusing your child? Compose yourself before you respond. Do not let your preoccupation with a chore or your changing moods because of other unrelated issues influence the way you react or respond to your child's behavior. Usually, taking a deep breath, counting to five, and clearing your mind before responding helps. This way, you can ensure that your responses are consistent, and you are not unintentionally confusing your little one. One more level to take care of is to tell all the concerned caregivers of your child what kind of behaviors require what kind of responses. Consistency at all levels is essential to help train your child into what is to be expected of them and what they are to expect from you. Consistency is a huge key element in the positive parenting approach.

Schedules

Make your own schedules and routines as a family and work to follow them consistently. You can work on different activities and items to include and work around in your family routine. Involve all the concerned caregivers for the child, and together work toward something that works for all of you in the interest of your child. You could set down rules to follow related to many different aspects like:

- Screen time
- Bedtime
- Sweets and sugar consumption
- Dinner table rules
- Discipline around the house
- Behavior when in company

These and many more like these can be a part of your own family guide book. Have this at a convenient place that your child can easily look up to, like a level wall space in the living room or a kitchen cabinet or fridge door, etc.

Ensure that not just you but also all the caregivers involved respect and follow your routine. If your child is put in a preschool, daycare, or in the care of a sitter, then make sure they are ready to respect and follow your routines with consistency. Any visiting relations, like grandparents, aunts, and uncles should also respect your routines. If you wouldn't want your child to be given sweets and sugars after 6 pm, or if you wouldn't want your child to have screen time on weekdays, then let it be known to the indulgent grandparents and aunts, too. Though letting it slip once in a blue moon is perfectly fine, it is important to not let it become a habit or an alternate option that your kids find easier to turn to.

Do not hesitate to advocate either for your child or your routines with the extended family or the chosen caregivers. If grandparents are going to stay for a while, and are not just visiting for a day, then it is important that you let them know what you expect of them in terms of your child's routine. If routines are broken time and again, and consistency is not maintained, then it will be even harder for you to get back in the groove and start over again with the schedules. Therefore, it is advisable to stick to them as best as possible, barring occasional slip-ups that are few and far between.

Manipulation and Toddlers

I must note here that I do not like the use of the word manipulation in this context. Toddlers are checking boundaries, being curious and creative in getting precisely what they want. That is all perfectly fine and age-appropriate. It is on us, their parents, to set the necessary boundaries and structure for them. So, for lack of a better word, I will be using the term manipulation but with a certain reservation.

One of the biggest hurdles parents may face with schedules and toddlers is the fact that toddlers are experts at manipulation. Their little minds are constantly looking for ways to bypass the routines set for them. From bedtime routines to meal-time routines, toddlers can try to manipulate adults into being lenient and bending a few rules.

For example, if your household has a rule of no sugars or sweets after 7 pm, your toddler will try hard to manipulate you into giving them desserts or ice cream at bedtime. If your child sleeps in a separate bed in a separate room, they may insist on sleeping in your bed with you. They will resist you trying to get them to brush their teeth before bed. Many times parents, feeling worn out and exasperated, give in to their demands and manipulations after trying to deny for a while. One thing to understand is toddlers are manipulative; it is in their nature. They don't do it with malice or any kind of ill intent. They do it in all their innocence and their need to have their way. They are inherently opposed to following limits and toeing the line. This is what causes them to manipulate parents and other adults into listening to them. This is where consistency helps. When you are being kind and firm, and are consistent with your routines, your child will learn that it is futile to try and change your mind. With time, they will come to enjoy their routines and will thank you for it as they grow. But now, what they need is a kind, firm, and consistent parent; all three together is the key.

CHAPTER 6:

TANTRUMS AND CHALLENGING BEHAVIORS

Before we delve into the deep, wide world of tantrums and misbehavior, and how to control and avoid them, it is important to understand why kids act as they do. What are the causes that lead them to behave questionably? Only when we have fully grasped the underlying issues for inexcusable behavior will we be able to work toward controlling and avoiding them altogether with more confidence and knowledge at our disposal.

Why Do Toddlers Have Tantrums?

The biggest reason for tantrums in toddlers is their struggle for self-control. Developmentally a toddler is looking for independence and autonomy. They are not fully adept at controlling and regulating their emotions. They are basically ego-centric, wanting to have everything go their way as per their choices. When things do not work as they want them to, they throw a fit or a tantrum to pressure us into accepting their train of thought.

As a parent, it is your job to guide them when they are facing these issues. Even before the situation has escalated into a tantrum, that is the time to act. Give them options that are suitable to them and which they can safely exercise their free will to choose from. Divert their minds to something completely different and unrelated and help them gain control of themselves. If your child is crying for a bowl of pasta, and you are offering them a bowl of cereal, divert their mind by offering them choices in the bowl they would like to use for their cereal. This takes away their attention from the pasta and guides them into the conversation at present in a gentle way.

Even after all you have tried and done, there might be times when nothing seems to work. This could be due to many reasons, sickness being one of them. At such times, you would simply have to accept that kids have bad days too, and simply handle it to the best of your ability and look forward to a healthy day to guide your child again.

Reasons For Misbehavior

We shall now see what different factors are that can adversely affect a child's behavior. One or more of these together can wreak havoc in a child's innocent mind, and they will find it difficult to cope with these changes and act in the way they know how to, by crying and drawing attention to themselves.

Sleep

Lack of sufficient sleep can make a child fussy and irritable. Children in the two to three year age group need at least 12 hours of sleep. If your child hasn't slept the required number of hours, then they are bound to be irritable and cranky at the most. Toddlers are still too young to truly understand that what they are facing is the need to fall asleep, so when sleep troubles them, and they are unable to understand it, they try to fight the onslaught of sleep by being irritable and cranky. When you are a positive and attentive parent, you would notice that your child hasn't slept their regular hours and you would work to put them to sleep as swiftly as possible.

Change in Routines

If your child is well-rooted in their regular schedules and routines, then an unexpected change can throw them off balance and cause them to be unreasonable. Things like a sudden visit to someplace, or people visiting and staying for a while, a birth in the family or some other family circumstances can alter the child's routine considerably. When a child is not surrounded by the known and expected routine, this could upset them easily. You would be left to wonder why an otherwise calm and collected child is suddenly upset and cranky. When you are observant, you would be able to identify that it is the change in schedules that has upset your child so.

Sickness

A mild sickness like a cold or a cough can also make your child's moods go haywire. Kids are not themselves when sick and it is understandable that their behavior would not be as expected too. If the sickness has gone on for a while, then you must be prepared to battle a long string of moodiness and irritability. The longer the sickness lasts, the longer it will take for your child to get back to normal behavior. But, do not fret about misbehavior or gaining bad habits in times of sickness. Let your child recuperate well and completely, and you can start over again with guidance and limits once your child is healthy and fine once more.

Hunger

One of the biggest and the most misunderstood reasons for misbehavior is hunger. Toddlers are too young to understand the concept of hunger. Though many kids are able to point at and ask for food when they wish to eat, it is not necessarily when they are hungry. Hunger throws them off path and they are unable to comprehend the state of their bodies. A normally quiet and calm child can potentially become cranky when faced with hunger. Especially if a child is used to having a snack at a fixed time and then doesn't eat it at their regular times, this can lead to hunger pangs which are difficult to perceive. Toddlers need little bites of some snack throughout the day. Their bodies aren't equipped to sustain on just three meals a day. Therefore, parents will notice that kids usually get irritable about three to four hours after a mealtime. If we measure by our standards, we might not realize that it is hunger they are facing and wouldn't address their hunger issues as such. These kids will behave irritably and throw fits for entirely unrelated and unreasonable things. For such kids, an occasional fruit, some kind of light salad, or a glass of milk or cookies can help calm them down and return them to their normal behavior.

The key here is being observant of your child's needs and their intake of food. If you are aware of how much and how often they eat, you can easily weed out unfavorable behaviors by simply giving them something to eat. It is advisable to keep simple snacks like your child's favorite fruits or energy bars handy so that you don't scramble about for healthy things to offer to your child when they are throwing a fit. If you are able to sense their being upset and are able to address it by offering something swiftly, that will help quell the tantrum before it blows over into something big and unmanageable.

Excess Screen Time

One of the new reasons that experts have come to understand in relation to questionable behaviors is being allowed too much screen time. Kids who are used to watching pictures and videos on the phone for long durations of time are known to become irritable when deprived. Children tend to get attracted to the moving colors and characters they watch on the screen. For them, it's like an alternate world, a way to counter boredom. But what this does instead is it might make kids lazy, lethargic, and irritable. A little screen time, on mobile phones, laptops, or ipads, is fine as long as it is limited and restricted to not more than half an hour per day. Do your best to ensure that kids below two to two and a half years do not watch anything. Set limits with regard to screen time that are followed by the whole family, something like no screen time on weekdays if that works for your family, or only half an hour every afternoon if that is more suited for you and your family.

Dealing with Common Challenging Behaviors

Let us now understand a few common challenging behaviors that are faced by parents most frequently. We will also see what is the best way to deal with each of these behaviors.

A vital point to remember before we venture into the world of challenging behaviors is to understand that several of these behaviors can easily be avoided by simply observing and taking care of your child. If your child is well-fed and well-rested, along with being given sufficient time to play, explore, and simply be independent and be themselves, many of these behaviors can be kept at bay.

List of Challenging Behaviors

Tantrums

Tantrums are when kids insist on following their way of doing things. Kids throw a fit when their wishes aren't met by crying, screaming, stomping their feet, and thrashing on the ground. These are common enough visuals for parents whose kids throw tantrums. So how are we supposed to deal with such behaviors?

Tantrums can be brought on by any of the reasons mentioned above. The key here is to stay calm. Repeat your expectations of them calmly, in a way they are able to understand. Act before the situation escalates into screaming and thrashing. Be open to being wrong, and accepting that perhaps some kind of a mistake or inability on your part resulted in this situation. When this happens and you have understood your lapses behind it, make it a point to accept it before your child with an apology. But, when it is pure stubbornness and unrelenting behavior on your child's part, you will need to be empathetic along with being firm. We shall see a few general tactics that can work on any kind of misbehavior in a later section.

Another point to keep in mind is to be consistent with your responses to the situation. If you have reacted in a certain way for a tantrum, then make sure to react the same way when this happens again in the future. Being consistent with your reactions to a similar kind of misbehavior is important to let no mixed messages reach your child about your approaches to their behaviors.

Hitting and Biting

Kids often resort to their versions of violence as a means of protest when things do not go their way. Kids also resort to hitting or biting others as a means of defense. In any scenario whatsoever, violence of any kind must never be permissible and should be censured and condemned strongly. But this too must be done keeping the tender age of a toddler in mind.

The first step when you encounter such behavior is to stay calm yourself. Obviously, it isn't going to be easy for you to digest and imagine that your little angel could resort to something of this kind too. Some parents, to counter their own embarrassment and shock, begin to panic and lose control of their emotions by resorting to violence themselves. This is wrong on many levels. You are, in a way, teaching kids it is fine to be violent in some situations. So, stay calm. You would be hurting the child more, emotionally as well as physically, by losing control yourself.

Try to get your child away from the scene. Remove the child from the situation wherever it is. If it is at the part that they are hitting or biting the other kids playing at the park, leave the park and get away from there with your child. If the child gets into a fight over a toy with their siblings and hit or bite them, then they must be removed from the room, the toy removed from them, forgone for a certain amount of time, and let them sit in their quiet place (see later chapters) or with their parent. The point here is to let it sink into the child that such actions will have consequences and it is most likely that they would have to let go or cut short whatever it was they were enjoying or wanted to enjoy.

Once you have your child calm and back to their usual collected selves, talk to them calmly about empathy and how their actions have hurt others. Explain to them why such violence is not permitted and how their actions have hurt you too. Make sure to talk in always positive language. Explain how we must use our hands for good and positive work. You could try and show them how hands and mouths are used for positive things like giving a kiss, a handshake, a hug, or a high five. Repeat your explanations and limits calmly and soothingly. This will take time, no doubt, but through patience and empathy you can help your child give up this harmful habit.

Defiance and Aggression

Without turning to tantrums or meltdowns, kids can still play defiant. They will deny and defy anything and everything you advise or instruct if it is not to their liking. Kids often resort to being aggressive and quarrelsome. One of the biggest issues in such scenarios is parents entering into power struggles with the child. Most parents take such defiance and aggression as a personal insult and find it difficult to come to terms with such behaviors. It is essential not to take these things personally and to treat these situations for what they truly are; your child's inability to handle emotions and be in control.

Try to stay as objective as possible, being the voice of reason for your little one. When they are upset and angry and refuse to listen to any advice, it is important to be calm and not lose your temper. They need your calmness to anchor them back. Your voice of reason will, in the end, be what calms them down. Give them options for what they can do instead. Give them healthy options to choose from. Stress what they can do instead of telling them what they cannot. Calmly repeat your expectations of them, as many times as they need.

Meltdowns and Crying

Meltdowns and excessive crying can be because they are upset. These need not necessarily result from a negative emotion or stubbornness. If the child is missing a loved one, a friend, or a grandparent, this can still cause them to breakdown into a meltdown. This is not so much a troubling matter with respect to their personality development as much as it is a matter of teaching them to handle and control their emotions.

The first thing to do is to affirm and acknowledge their feelings of being hurt or upset. Name their emotions for them so they know what it is they are feeling. "I see you are crying and are upset. You must be really sad," or something along these lines.

Whether the upset is a result of either stubbornness or missing someone, perhaps, let them cry it out calmly. Wait till they are quiet on their own. Do not press them or force them into becoming quiet. This will only suppress their emotions for the time being, which will be difficult to control once they are crying again. You could let them release their emotions in their quiet place (see chapter 8). Once they are calm and not crying anymore, you can talk to them to soothe their feelings. Kiss or hug them to let them know you care and understand their situation too. You could help them control their emotions by teaching them different breathing techniques and urging them to look for positives in every situation.

Refusing to Nap

Many kids hate to go to sleep. Many resort to stubborn behavior, crying, or other methods to try and delay going to bed. You could counter this behavior by adopting a reward system in your house. Use a reward chart or a points chart to encourage sleeping on time. Include sleep times in your daily schedules and make it a point to follow them thoroughly with firmness. To encourage your child to look forward to sleeping times, you could give them options such as to allow them to choose their own music or book while going to sleep. Give them responsibilities that will make them want to work to emulate an adult by dimming the lights each night, for example. Set limits or expectations for the last time when the child must lie down on the bed, regardless of whether they sleep or not. If it is staying alone that they fear, then you can remain in the room along with them, within their vision, till the time they fall asleep. Gradually move farther from their bed but still stay in the room where they can see you. You can then move into a position where, though they cannot see you, they know that you are present. You could put a chair someplace away from their bed and engage yourself in a book. Continue this until you are able to fade away from the room and your child is comfortable with you being away.

Potty Regression

This is a common issue with kids of many different age groups. Kids usually believe they would rather be doing something interesting or playing something worthwhile instead of spending minutes together in the toilet. This may be more in the case of kids who are physically active and love playing games. Quiet and calm children do not usually display this problem. A simple solution could be to introduce a reward chart to encourage them to answer their natural calls and urges as they should and on time. If your child is not yet potty-trained, wait until they are ready to start the training. Potty regression is a problem with kids who are not potty trained also. One reason for this behavior could also be because parents are too particular and nag their children excessively about using the potty. To counter the continuous nagging, they become rebellious and refuse to use the potty. Encourage your child when they use the toilet and validate their feelings when they are upset, angry, or busy and not interested in using the potty. Be empathetic and gently encourage them when they respond positively.

To avoid such challenging behaviors as a parent, it is your duty to provide your child with good healthy food and sufficient sleep and resting time along with time to play and be active. Give them healthy choices when you take something away from them. Set behavioral expectations for your child with clarity and known rewards or consequences. Prepare your child well in advance in case of planned outings or sudden transitions. Keep in mind that toddlers are too young to understand time as we do. Rushing them with their activities or games because we are 'running late' is a disservice to them. They do not yet have an idea of what being late means. This rushing through of their routine can also result in meltdowns and tantrums.

Keeping calm and not losing your own emotions is necessary to maintain control of the situation too. Only when you are calm will you be able to think with clarity and do the right thing by your child.

Avoiding Misbehavior

What we have seen until now is how to handle the various ways in which a child might misbehave. We have seen what to do in such situations to defuse it and calm your child effectively. What we will see now is how to avoid such situations altogether.

Diversions

This is a great tactic to help avoid situations that can potentially turn problematic. If you are out with the whole family, you naturally wouldn't want your child to display their prowess at throwing tantrums. When you sense the slightest bit of displeasure or a hint of upset in your child, take immediate control of the situation by diverting your child's mind. Children are innocent and extremely divertible. Use this to your advantage. In order to effectively divert your child's attention from the subject of contention that has resulted in the tantrum, talk of something that is completely different. Talk and draw their attention to something entirely unrelated, like, for example, if you are at a restaurant, and your child begins to throw a tantrum for some ice cream, talk to them about the many different lights and decorations present around the restaurant, or what you will do in the coming holidays as a family. The point here is to take their attention away from whatever it is they are wishing after.

It is not to deny them what could easily be given to them, but rather to encourage them to respect the boundaries that their parents have set for them. If what they wish for is something that can easily be given to them without causing any negative effects in their routines or disturb their boundaries, then parents, by all means, can go ahead and give it to them promptly. But doing so after a certain amount of time has passed going to and fro in a power struggle with the child is highly inadvisable. A parent must be able to swiftly decide whether the requested item is fit to be allowed at the moment and act accordingly to avoid unnecessary aggression on the child's part.

Diversion tactics are a great way to control a situation that can otherwise get out of hand easily. The key here is to recognize a potentially deteriorating situation quickly and act swiftly.

Appreciation

Appreciation is one of the key things a child of any age feeds on. This is especially true in the case of toddlers. Appreciation is key to any child's healthy personality development. A child denied this basic emotional need could grow into a bitter personality who is unable to see the good in others, just as others were unable to spot the goodness in them.

Make it a point to appreciate and acknowledge whatever little good your child does. Praise them for every little achievement they accomplish. What could toddlers do to earn such consistent praise? They bring you a cup from the table, praise them. They help you sort their toys and books out, praise them. For every single helpful activity they do, praise them. Praise them for being good and behaving well too. Do they follow their routines, their schedules correctly? Do they do all their activities? All these things deserve praise. For toddlers, praise can never be excessive. Encourage them as much as possible at every reason you can find.

Now what does this do? Praising your child gives them confidence in themselves. Appreciation urges your child to do the good so as to gain your praise time and again. This is a good enough motivation to be good for a toddler. As a child grows and acquires empathy toward others, they would slowly replace their motivations for their actions from gaining your praise to actually doing something meaningful for others. But at this age, appreciation is an excellent tool to lend them confidence and push them toward staying good and behaving admirably.

Are Your Needs Met?

When we are tired or sick, we are easily frustrated by the simplest of things. A thing which couldn't have more than annoyed us otherwise or perhaps even prompted a bout of laughter out of us normally, can easily cause us to lose our heads when we are not our best selves. Taking a moment to pause and think if it is indeed a serious misbehavior or is it our own frustration leading us on can be a good idea in such situations. When your needs are met and you are well-rested and fed, you are more in control of the situation. It will be easier to control your emotions and compose yourself when your other parameters are met. Therefore, before you blow off your steam or take an action to avoid what you think is a misbehavior or scold your child for the same, take a moment to evaluate your own conditions first to ensure you aren't blaming your child for what could be your own problem.

Having a Kid-Friendly Environment

You place the valuable glass vase from Japan that your mother gifted to you on a low corner table in the living area. Your little toddler who is full of energy and is always running and bumping around, bumps into the table and knocks it to the ground. Your precious piece of treasure is strewn across the floor in tiny pieces. It's true your child probably shouldn't have been running around in the house like that. But, what could you expect from a little child who is not yet three years old? So instead of blowing your head off before the child and accusing the little one of ruining your treasure, you must take a moment to see who really was responsible here. If that vase was glass, and on top of that was precious to you, would it not have been better to simply place it on a higher shelf that your child can't reach or bump into? Several parents fail to maintain a kid-friendly environment around the house. When this results in accidents, mishaps or injuries, parents are often quick to blame the child in question and not realize their own glaring mistake in the whole matter. It is important that you have all dangerous, harmful, precious, or important things out of the way of the children in the house. From scissors, needles, matchsticks, lighters, glass decorations, to important documents, pieces of jewelry, or other such essentials, keep them far away, out of the reach of your toddlers. It is always better to be cautious and safe than to be sorry and sad later on.

Take a Break Together

Sometimes it so happens that both you and your child are so overwhelmed with the stress of toeing the line and following the limits that scenarios can get intense and too stressful. Excessive meltdowns, daily tantrums, and continued irritability are signs that perhaps your toddler needs a break. This could be due to many reasons. Their health, insufficient sleep, or hunger, can all cause such imbalances. Mostly such behaviors are common in children who are just coming out of a long illness. In such situations, instead of wading through stressful muddled waters every single day, you could both take a break and head out somewhere peaceful. A simple day at the park, a picnic, a movie night, or a sleepover that you both have together at a friend's or relative's place, can all work wonders for your child's temperament and your sanity.

Reassurance

As we discussed earlier, kids at times are only looking for means to feel loved and gain your attention. You can satisfy this need of theirs by offering reassurances to them from time to time. Through special activities that you can do together or through verbal demonstrations, you can reassure your child that you love them and they truly are the center of your world. A timely hug, a goodnight kiss, or some shared ice cream on the sofa can all become special moments that strengthen their belief that they are important enough for you.

Avoid Abstracts

Kids are straightforward and simple, and they understand straightforward and simple the best. Make it a point to keep your instructions and advice simple and straightforward, too. Do not include vague and abstract instructions of what you wish them to understand and follow. Parents use advice and admonishments such as "be careful," "sit properly," "stand properly," "run cautiously" and so on. For a two- or three-year-old toddler, what do careful, properly, cautiously even mean? They are too young, and their language still undeveloped to a large extent to understand the abstract meanings of your instructions. Instead of saying so, you could spell out exactly what you wish them to do to make things more straightforward, easy to understand and appropriate for their age, like saying, "Do not stand on the edge of the bench. You could fall.", "We sit with our legs down on the floor instead of on the sofa." These are more direct and specific as to what you want them to do and correct in their behavior or actions. Older kids are better at understanding abstract, but for toddlers, it would be difficult, so simply stay away from using abstract sentences.

Give Them Time

Just like we need time to compose ourselves before we face an issue, children need time too. We might take deep breaths, drink a sip of water, or try sitting down when we are angry or when we feel we are losing control. Similarly, give your children a moment and space to compose themselves. Doing this does two things. One, it gives them the time to gather themselves and bring their emotions under control, and two, it lets them know that you respect them and are willing to stand by and wait for them to be ready.

Saying something like, "It's all right. Take a deep breath just like mommy taught you. We'll talk this over when you are calm and ready", or "I'll wait until you are ready to talk again. Take the flower breath, it might help you." (More on breathing exercises for toddlers in Chapter 8). Giving this space and time for your children to compose themselves can become a very positive influence on how they treat others when sad, upset, or angry. It can go on to become a vital personality trait if they are able to give space and show the same empathy to others as was shown to them.

Having a Sense of Humor

If we can draw ourselves back into the background of our day to day lives and observe our toddler's activities as a bystander, we are sure to laugh out loud on more than one occasion. Toddlers and their antics are cute. It is just that we aren't in a position to laugh things off at the moment, because all we see is how much trouble their actions can cause us. You see your toddler trying to fill themselves a bowl of cereal and add milk to it, spilling more than half of it on the ground. You do not pause and take in the absurdity or the innocence of the act. Instead, the only thing you notice is the mess of cereal and the spilled milk on the floor. That is what turns this into an instance of bad behavior, and you become angry. Twenty years from that moment, wouldn't we be laughing it off remembering how your toddler looked, perched on the stool, with a look of deep concentration, with cereal and milk everywhere? If we can laugh then, why can't we laugh it off now? There is extra work and cleaning to do, no doubt, but if you could enjoy that moment and laugh it off along with your toddler instead of telling them off for trying something so innocent, wouldn't that be so much better? You will have to clean the mess anyhow, why not do it laughing and smiling instead of angry and frowning? Laughing it off will also help your child from feeling embarrassment or guilt. You could later sit with your child and explain how to go about things or come to you when they need something, but at that moment, have a sense of humor and lighten the mood.

Set Realistic Expectations

Many misbehaviors and mishaps can be avoided simply by setting realistic expectations from your children. Do not expect your toddler to learn everything and understand the very first time they are told something. Just like they need a year to learn to walk, another year to learn to talk, they will need time and effort both on your part and theirs to understand what is acceptable and what is not. Just because they are now able to talk and express themselves, we cannot expect them to be completely ready for displaying socially acceptable and appropriate behavior. They will need time and repeated instructions to help them understand what you expect of them. For this, it is necessary that you set the bar low for them and let your expectations be age-appropriate. If you expect your two-year-old to willingly share their teddy bear with a visiting cousin, then you are indeed expecting too much. Toddlers of three years old, too, find it difficult to share their things with others, so expecting this of a two-year-old is nearly impossible. Set realistic expectations and you will be less disappointed when they do not fulfill those expectations.

Vents for Unspent Energy

Children, toddlers especially, are little balls of energy. They need regular outlets to let these energy buildups out. This is one of the reasons why you will find a toddler running and jumping all day long and still feel ready to burst with energy by night time. When they get no means to spend this stored up energy, they resort to any action they find suitable to release their active energies. From running around the house, climbing on cupboards, running up and down the stairs, to throwing things around, or jumping on furniture, these are all means that kids resort to to expend their energies. This is a developmental requirement for toddlers to run about and play actively. For this very reason, it is important to provide suitable ways your toddler can actively play throughout the day. Take them to the park, or out in the yard or the garden and simply let them run and play. Ideally, toddlers need at least two hours of active play per day. When this need for physical activity isn't met, toddlers react adversely and resort to misbehavior through unsuitable means and activities. If you notice your child being excessively active, or too full of energy at bedtime, take note of how much physical exertion they had during the day. This way, you can make suitable changes to their day time routines to include physical activity so they do not have to resort to undesirable actions.

How Connections Help in Correcting Misbehavior

The importance of forming connections truly cannot be stressed enough. Before you move to correct any misbehavior of your child, it is extremely important to form a connection first. Connections help you form a validating attachment with your child. It is like telling your child, "I love you but you can't have it." Connections are not just meaningful at the time of misbehavior but also when the child is happy and well. Make regular efforts to form a connection with your child through different activities that encourage healthy conversations. A few such options are listed below.

Special Time

Allot a special time for connecting with your child. Let this time be expressly for talking and having fun with your child. Let your child speak and share their feelings with you, while you simply listen to them with great attention. Play games, do simple crafts or cook a salad with your child in this special time. Work toward making this time truly special and memorable for your child.

Problem-Solving

Involve your child in simple problem-solving situations. Get your toddler to give you suggestions for simple household or family issues, like if you are redecorating, your child can help you decide where to place the magazine basket, or where to put a decorative piece around the living room, something simple and ordinary that can make them feel special through helping and contribution. Even if their suggestions are not worth following, still encourage and thank them for giving their opinions and tell them how grateful you are to have them help you with solving problems. With time, these little problem-solvers will be interested in solving actual problems that matter to you, them, and the whole family. Problem-solving is a skill that you can help develop in your child from as soon as the toddler age.

Family Time

Let this time be an occasion where the whole family connects. Adults and older children can contribute to the family time by presenting issues and providing solutions to problems. You could also include a few fun and interactive sessions during this time that involve all the family members, and this is where your toddler can contribute. Let them recite a poem, tell a story, or provide some kind of entertainment through games or such. Involving them in family meetings will help them notice and learn from their older siblings and also give a means to connect with the whole family. This family time tradition will become a treasured time for them as they grow.

Hugs

Give regular hugs to your child. Many times, a simple hug is often enough to resolve many issues and dilute stressful situations. A hug tells your child you love them and care for them. Make it a point to give them hugs at random unexpected times along with regular specific times such as bedtimes or morning hours.

A child who feels connected is less likely to disobey, feel disconnected, or misbehave in any way. It is the answer to several behavioral problems children of all ages experience. If you can make genuine efforts to connect with your child, it will show its positive effects in a lot less time than yelling or punishing can do.

Understanding Power Struggles and Why Kids Don't Listen

Power struggles are when you and your child get into a back and forth argument where each is trying to establish their power and supremacy. Toddlers and older kids too, have minds of their own and are reluctant to let you boss them around. You, on the other hand, being the obvious figure of authority, are averse to letting your position go. This then results in heated and intense arguments with each trying hard to prove who is right and has the most influence. Such power struggles are unhealthy and undesirable for both you and your child. This basically stems from the simple reason that your child doesn't listen to you. But why they don't listen can again be due to a number of reasons. For toddlers, these reasons are more in number, seeing the really small attention span they have. Let us see one after the other what it could be that results in your children not listening to you and what steps you can take to counter them.

- They are copying. This could be a simple enough reason of why such back and forth arguments occur between you and your child. Imagine if a child regularly sees and observes their caregivers, babysitters, you, or your spouse arguing with someone or the other, and imbibes it as a good enough model to follow. The next you notice your child is repeating what they saw and talking back to you just as they saw you or others do with each other. Little kids are like sponges. They soak up what they see and observe. Needless to say, they are excellent imitators and they love to copy. What you are seeing in your child as an extreme case of disrespectful behavior or bad adult talk, could only be them copying the adults around them. In such cases, instead of scolding or lecturing them, simply sit them down and explain why such things are unacceptable.

Remember, not only do you have to speak to them nicely but also take care to speak around them nicely. Mention your preference for what kind of talk is acceptable or not acceptable to everyone who is in contact with your child. Their caregivers, babysitters, relatives or friends watching them must all understand and realize what kind of speech to maintain around your child.

- One reason your child might not be paying attention to what you are saying could be that they are simply bored. When their attention is on things that they would rather be doing than listening to you, then they are bound to ignore you. When they are more interested in getting back to playing with slime, and you are explaining to them about the importance of keeping their toys in their places, naturally, your child will be bored and will not pay attention to you. To counter this issue, make it a point to first get their attention and make sure nothing distracting is waiting for them, then perhaps they will be more attentive to what you are trying to say.

- Another reason why children might not listen is when you take too long to come to the point. You lecture on and on with no end in sight, then tiny toddlers with their tinier attention spans are bound to zone out of the conversation. Try to keep things crisp and short. Do not babble about how you were in your childhood, how you struggled and how yet you were a model child. Your child isn't interested in the story right now, not when they are still a toddler. Instead, get right to the point and put your expectations before them.

- When you use words in your conversations that your little toddler either doesn't understand or finds insulting, then you have lost them from the conversation again. Keep your words and sentences simple and age-appropriate, along with being mindful of how your toddler takes these words. For example, "Ella, don't be ridiculous. We can't go to the park now," or "I want to see the living room immaculate and all the silverware pristine and sparkling." In the first sentence calling your child ridiculous can throw them out of the conversation. They wouldn't pay attention to anything you tell them after that one sentence. In the second instance, they are out of the conversation as soon as they hear the words immaculate and pristine. When you are talking about chores and cleaning, what possible interest can the child have in getting to know the meaning of words they find difficult to understand? It is easier, therefore, to simply tune you out and let you talk without listening.

- You don't follow through with your limits. When you set limits and boundaries for your child and have resulting consequences in place, yet you do not follow through on these limits and their consequences, it gives kids a license to repeat their misbehavior again and again. This could be a strong reason why toddlers don't listen to you because they know you won't follow through with whatever you are setting up for them.

- If you have a habit of yelling at your children and you yell frequently enough, then toddlers take it to believe that is precisely what means you are serious. When you are talking calmly to them, they are less likely to pay attention because, for them, you are not serious enough about the issue if you are not yelling. To counter this issue, stop yelling at your children altogether. Even at times that you feel yelling is necessary and it would be easier to hold their attention, hold yourself back and have a little patience. Compose yourself, count to five, and then talk. If you are already in the habit of yelling at your kids, then this might take time. But it is better to get rid of this damaging habit as yelling is never a good idea.

- One very obvious reason why your children seem as though they aren't listening is because they truly aren't listening. At times, kids are too engrossed and immersed in what they are doing. Solving the puzzle correctly without a single misplaced piece is obviously more important to them than listening to you. And they are too preoccupied to even have heard you talking. For this reason, first gather their attention and then begin your talk. Only when they leave their activity and look at you, should you begin talking. Either through calling their name or by making a sound, like tapping on the table or knocking on the door, make sure you first have their attention before you talk.

One way to ensure your children listen to you is to talk less or talk softly. When you speak to your child and find their attention slipping, try whispering. Talking softly or whispering is known to get their attention better than shouting or yelling at them. Kids snap into attention when you whisper because they find it different and intriguing. Use this to your advantage when you wish them to give you full attention. Also, try to act more than you talk. Use fewer words and more actions to convey your message. Instead of telling your toddler repeatedly to pick up toys, simply lead them to the scattered toys and say gently, "These toys are all scattered. Let's pick them up. Would you like to race?" When fewer words are followed by actions, they are more likely to be listened to.

CHAPTER 7:

THE POWER OF EMPATHY

Being an empathetic parent is the best gift a parent can give to their child. Your empathy for your child will let them understand that you actually 'get them'. Just like adults need someone to show confidence in them and acknowledge their feelings, so do young kids, especially toddlers. We need an understanding shoulder to lean on and cope with our time of distress. That shoulder will only be a support when the person understands where we are coming from and what is the reason for our present situation.

Toddlers are no different. They need us, parents, to be those understanding shoulders for them. We can become such strong support for them only by showing empathy. It is essential for kids that we understand them and their needs. For toddlers, their emotional needs and their feelings are of paramount importance. For us, a crying, whining, screaming, thrashing child might be just that, a child behaving undesirably. More so when according to us, they are doing so for no real reason and for 'nothing'. But for them, it is hugely important. How many times have we encountered parents who defend their ignorance of their child's needs by saying it was 'nothing'? For us, it indeed might be nothing, but to them, it is as important as the world.

Being empathetic toward your child gives you the space to see the world through their eyes. It makes space for your feelings without any judgment. Empathy is the great affirmation that toddlers need that tells them, "I understand how you are feeling. It's alright. Your feelings matter to me."

Empathy lets your child feel connected to you. It gives them a sense of belonging and security. They will be more at ease knowing you are someone who understands them. This will bring more confidence in your relationship with your child. Children who have empathetic parents are easier to "manage" and work around. They live with the knowledge that they have support to fall back on bad days. If the parent is always critical and lacks empathy, the child will retreat within themselves. Such parents may be unable to foster a relationship based on trust and confidence with their kids. Such children will build resentment toward parents as time goes by. Empathy gives them the validation their feelings need.

The very first step to validation is being welcoming of their mistakes. You are not accepting their behavior, rather welcoming the fact that they are humans and will make mistakes just like you do. We are taught from our early childhood that mistakes are bad, and the ones committing mistakes are wrong. We are taught that making an error is akin to failure. What we need to realize is that children are innocent. They aren't bad, they are pure. But when we are not welcoming of their mistakes, we are saying the exact opposite to them. When you are accusatory in your approach, kids resort to hiding and covering up their mistakes because they fear you. Hiding mistakes can never be a good idea, as one lie would need a hundred more to hide it. This is not a good trait to encourage in your child. When you hide a wrongdoing, you can neither rectify it nor can you learn from it to avoid it in future. Instead, be welcoming of their mistakes, guiding them gently as to how they can correct them with empathy. This is what validation gives them; a chance to get back up from their failures, learn from them, and try not to repeat them.

Validation versus Acceptance

Many parents confuse validating their child's behavior with accepting their behavior as correct. These aren't the same. Validation is simply to affirm the feelings of your child as something worth taking note of. You give their feelings the respect they deserve without brushing them off as inconsequential and meaningless. One of the biggest criticisms of the theory of empathy is that it encourages the child into feeling confident about their mistakes and urges them to continue their bad behavior. This also isn't true.

Validation is not equal to condoning bad behavior. You are validating the way your child feels but not the way your child behaves. While you are being empathetic toward your child by telling them how you understand their feelings and as to why they are angry or upset, you also firmly establish how you do not support or condone their bad behavior. See the following as an example.

A three-year-old is upset that her older brother has finished her orange juice. They both get into an argument, and she throws the empty juice carton at her brother who ducks, and the empty box lands on the side table holding crockery, breaking a glass quarter plate and smashing it to pieces on the floor. Here their quarrel and argument has resulted in a broken plate and the danger of strewn glass pieces all over the kitchen floor. Obviously, any caregiver would be angry. She was in the right by being upset, but was the ensuing argument and throwing things appropriate? How must the parent react? How would you react?

What the child needs here is for us to understand that firstly she is simply three years old. Just two years older from being a no-idea-what's-happening infant. Just one year older from being able to talk. That is still a very young age for us to be taking them to task. So what do we do? What that child needs is a hug and a rub on the back that tells them you understand. If it is a sensitive child, they would be crying even before you look at them. A tougher child is bound to melt into your arms and cry when you give that hug. Why is this so? Because at this tender age, kids are too innocent to foster any real animosity or negativity. Their own guilt will bring those tears on. At this point, they are too overwhelmed by the loss of their juice and then the loss of their own emotions. You would only be hurting them more by scolding or yelling at them.

Once they have calmed down, the crying has subsided, and they are able to look at you without being uncomfortable, now is the time to gently tell them it was wrong. By this time, they know that already. But you have to lay down the rules when your child is calm and in a receptive enough state to listen and acknowledge what you are saying.

"I know you were upset. You were angry your brother drank your juice. But, dearest, what just happened wasn't fine. You mustn't throw things at each other. We talk and solve our problems. We do not throw things at each other. This could have seriously hurt someone."

This much is enough to let the message sink in. But this message will only get in their minds when you have held them and rubbed their backs, giving them that much-needed hug. That simple, empathetic gesture broke the barrier between the parent and the child. It is what made the child more accepting of their own follies and the given advice. Of course, you mustn't forget the older brother or his part in this whole scenario, but for now, our concentration was the vulnerable little girl of three.

Validation is like saying I get how you are feeling. I don't agree with what you have done, but I understand why you have done it. You can and must set behavioral limits while being empathetic at the same time.

Strategies on How to Empathize With Your Toddler

If you are looking to be empathetic to your child's feelings, there are a few things to keep in mind to effectively convey the right message of understanding.

- Bring yourself to their level. Either bend down or kneel so that you both are at the same level.
- Look your child in the eye and truly listen to them. Put away any phones or electronics, or any other chore that you might be doing, to give them your undivided attention.
- Reflect and repeat what they say. It is always a good thing to repeat what they tell you back to them. Doing this accomplishes two things. It tells them you have understood what they are saying and also opens for them a chance to correct you if you have in any way misunderstood them.
- Describe how they look and give them words to help them tell you how they feel. For example, you may say, "You are pounding the table with your fists, you look angry!"
- Ask them appropriate questions so you know you are understanding them correctly and validating their feelings and not the feelings you have chosen for them. For example, you might say something like, "You look sad, are you sad?" And then you let them agree or disagree.
- While being empathetic, do not criticize, judge, or try to solve their problems for them. Doing this would only defeat the purpose of being empathetic in the first place.

- Do not tell them, "You are feeling sad, so this is what you need…"
- Do not tell them, "Stop crying. If you go on crying, everyone will think you are a cry baby."
- Do not tell them, "You are always upset at the table during dinner."

Validating your child's feelings is just as important as teaching them manners and ethics. For toddler years, this is even more important as at this tender age they are unaware of the complex emotions a human being is capable of feeling, and all that they undergo is bound to be overwhelming for an innocent mind. This age needs the most amount of validation and empathy to help the child learn the range of their own emotions and how to handle them.

Have a Meaningful Talk

Sometimes all you need is to sit and talk. Make it a point to have at least one meaningful conversation with your child every day. What you could do is have such a conversation at bedtime with your child. Before or after storytime, you could sit with your child and talk about your day. Then ask them about theirs and simply listen. It is remarkable how much a child is willing to share when you are ready to listen. Ensure that you end your conversation on a happy note that leaves your child smiling. Be it a joke, a funny story, a funny incident from your day at the office, or anything else, let the last memory of you be a happy one for your child as they drift off to sleep.

Having such sharing sessions is a step toward empathy. It will help you strengthen your relationship with your child and enrich the trust factor between you both. This is a valuable asset to have in your relationship as a parent as your child grows. With time, as your child grows and starts school, this very session will come in handy. Your child will be more forthcoming and trusting of you to share their day's happening with you every day. This ease of conversation is what any parent desires, and you can have it too through a little empathy.

CHAPTER 8:

MINDFULNESS AND AUTONOMY FOR YOUR TODDLER

Mindfulness for your toddler means to bring their attention to what they are experiencing at a given moment. You aim at giving them valuable actionables that they can use to experience their present moments with complete acceptance without fear of being judged as right or wrong. A few simple strategies can help your child to calm themselves and get back to normalcy after a difficult or stressful situation. If your child is crying, having a meltdown, or throwing a tantrum, these mindfulness strategies will help them to be calm and collected once again.

A Quiet Place

Traditional parenting involves a concept of a place for 'time-out'. This is where a child is sent for having misbehaved in some way. This is a means of severe punishment through a sort of boycott for the child. The child isn't allowed to speak or interact with others and, in more extreme cases, may even be asked to sit in a corner facing the wall. This is cruel on many levels, more so for a toddler. The young two- or three-year-old is already overwhelmed with the jumble of emotions running through them. They are too young to understand and sort out what it is they are feeling; sadness, anger, jealousy, impatience, irritability, all these feelings are new for them. To this, if you add the feeling of being punished by having to sit with no human interaction for a certain amount of time, you can imagine how character-breaking that scenario might be for the child.

Though the concept of letting the child calm down by staying aloof and away from the situation that caused trouble in the first place has merit, still the way it is practically implemented, and the intention behind the action entirely changes the effects it has. Instead, if you can have a place specifically for your child to vent, cry, and gradually calm themselves without the additional feeling of being punished, then that would indeed be admirable. This is what a quiet place is. Build a quiet place for your child that they can use to expel their emotions and come back to normalcy.

How Is 'Quiet Place' Different From 'Time-Out'

A time-out place could be any corner in the house that is simply away from the situation or place of misbehavior. There is no thought given to the surroundings or comfort of the child as long as the child is away from the scene of misbehavior. A quiet place is entirely different. This is a specific place in the house, preferably a room or spot that the child likes. You give special attention to placing different things around in this one spot that are sure to calm, soothe, or interest the child.

Going to the quiet place is the child's choice. You simply present the option of calming themselves in their corner. Accepting your suggestion and making use of this corner to become calm is entirely up to them. This is not the case with time-out. In a time-out, the child is forced to leave and move to a corner as a punishment for their misbehavior.

The quiet place must be a safe place for your toddler. It should contain things that they will find soothing and comfortable. Place a few blankets, pillows, a comfy chair, and their favorite soft toys or stuffed animals that they find comforting to have around. One good idea is to place a soothing or diverting visual object to help them calm down. Things like a colorful rotating light bulb, an aquarium, or a glass pot with interesting fish, a 3D display of some kind, etc. It is not advisable to place food in the quiet place as not to teach your child to deal with their emotions through food, but do not forget to place a bottle of water for them to drink. The point is to give them a safe place to relax and switch back to normal. Keep in mind to always keep your child in the line of your vision so that you are able to monitor them from afar so that they remain safe and do not injure themselves accidentally.

Providing a quiet-place is a self-regulating emotional tool in the positive parenting toolkit. It is an effective way to teach your child to self-soothe and let their emotions out or cool themselves when they are upset or angry. A quiet place will ensure that your child is calm and relaxed before reasoning with an adult about their behavior. After a little time in a quiet place, a child will be more agreeable and receptive to what the parent is trying to teach or tell them.

Breathing Techniques

One other excellent way to help your child in times of stress and teach them to self-soothe is to employ breathing techniques. There are several breathing techniques that you can use to calm them when they are upset or angry. Teach them these exercises when they are happy and interested. Do not attempt to teach them breathing exercises in the midst of a meltdown, as this would not be helpful at all, and can, in fact, make them irritable and annoyed.

Teach them these techniques when they are in a playful mood and make a game out of it to inspire interest. You can do these exercises along with them to give them company and assure them of its benefits.

The Flower Breath

This breathing technique is similar to smelling a flower. You breathe in through your nose and out through your mouth. An imaginary flower smelling game can be useful in teaching kids this exercise.

The Bunny Breath

This breathing technique involves taking three quick breaths or sniffs through your nose and exhaling in one long breath through your mouth. The three quick sniffs are akin to a bunny sniffing things around and hence the name. As your child gets the hang of this exercise, you could train them to exhale slowly. The slower the exhale, the more effective this technique will be in calming them.

The Snake Breath

This is when you breathe through your nose and out through your mouth with a slow hissing sound from between your teeth. The sound is similar to the hiss of a snake and the kids would enjoy playing around and learning this exercise while pretending to be a snake!

Blow Out The Candle Breath

This is when you pretend you are blowing out a candle. Let your child imagine a birthday cake with candles and practice blowing them off. You inhale through your nose but exhale through your mouth through an 'o' in a slow whoosh as though blowing out a candle. You could draw a cake with candles or use props to teach kids this exercise.

The Roller Coaster Breath

This technique involves following a roller coaster path or track to frame your breathing around. You make use of a roller coaster track drawn on a paper, which is basically an asymmetrical design of uneven highs and lows. You start from one end of the line and breathe following the pattern or the track. You inhale on the highs and exhale on the lows. As the roller coaster moves up you inhale and exhale as it moves down. The inclines and declines being uneven, your breathing would be the same. Doing this gives you control over your breathing. This is a useful technique to teach your kids, though very young kids might find it difficult to follow the instructions for this exercise. But once mastered, this is an excellent way to help calm yourself with controlled breathing.

The Square Breath

For this technique, you would need to participate and demonstrate to your child how to breathe using the square breath. Count till three as you breathe in, then hold your breath and count till three, then count till three again as you exhale and hold your breath and count again till three. This four-step process is what gives it this name. If the child needs a little assistance with understanding it, you could encourage them to draw a line in the air at each step, forming a square before them. You could even simply hold up your fingers for the counting and encourage them to do the same for each step. Repeated breathing through this exercise is a good way to stay calm and regulate one's emotions.

Sphere Breath

This is a very simple exercise that kids can easily master on their own. You simply connect your fingertips to form a ball or sphere with your hands. As you inhale, you enlarge the sphere, and as you exhale, you flatten your hands to deflate the sphere. It is like filling air in your belly and exhaling out slowly. The sphere with the help of fingertips is to simply help a child relate to the exercise.

The Ocean Breath

This is an interesting breathing technique. You take a deep breath through your nose and with your mouth tightly shut, exhale while you make a deep sound at the base of your throat. This is like the sound of an ocean and hence the name.

The Shoulder Roll Breath

This is an awesome trick not just to calm your breathing but also to relax your upper torso muscles as you do this exercise. As you inhale, roll your shoulders up to your ears and roll them back down again as you exhale.

The Mountain Breath

In this technique, you raise your hands as high over your head as you can. You join your palms and bring your hands down as you exhale.

These exercises are helpful not just for children but also for adults. These are useful tips to teach your child to calm themselves. By continued practice after a sufficient amount of time, you will notice your kids making use of these techniques without your help, too. They will be so accustomed to using these techniques that they will opt for these calming techniques unconsciously, too.

Feeling Charts

Feeling charts are an innovative way to teach kids to understand their own emotions as well as others. These charts have drawings or pictures depicting various emotions helping the kids to relate. Kids are then encouraged to identify and acknowledge their emotions from these pictures. This little exercise helps kids to name their feelings. Emotional literacy through vocabulary or feeling facial expressions, is a good way to encourage kids to understand and regulate their emotions.

Use a feeling chart with well-labeled feeling expressions that children are easily able to identify and name. Either place this chart in your child's safe place or their calming quiet place, or keep one handy to use anywhere by getting one laminated for extended use.

These charts can help a toddler name their feelings and also allow the parent to coach the child appropriately through their difficult feelings. Children will find it easy and also interesting to let you know how they are feeling all through the day using this emotional vocabulary. This can help them navigate difficult situations so that they do not escalate into challenging behaviors, and kids are able to replace such behaviors with their respective feeling. This is important if you would like the child to be able to control their emotions on their own when upset and not allow things to get out of hand.

Encouraging Self-Reliance and Self-Sufficiency

Independent, self-sufficient children must be the dream of every parent. When children are able to perform various tasks on their own and use their own thoughts and decision-making abilities to make sound decisions, they can be known to be developing and growing remarkably well. This is what parents aim to achieve. This admirable trait which the kids are naturally inclined toward gets squashed and suppressed by our many fears as parents and by our reluctance to give up our hold on their lives through the means of various disciplinary methods. But the same admirable traits can be encouraged by following a few important things that can lead your child to age-appropriate independence.

Questions and Curiosity

Toddlers are curious by nature. They love to explore the world and learn from what they observe around them. They are too observant and perceptive, at times more than the adults who look after them. Their curious nature leads them into asking numerous questions to the adults around them.

How is the fan able to run with the switch? Where is the rain coming from? Where did the moon go in the morning? And so many similar and other very incomprehensible questions that can quiet baffle an adult. Do not stifle their curiosity by brushing off their questions as inconsequential, unnecessary, or unwanted. Let them ask questions and learn and explore on their own. Toddlers with their infinite curiosity are little scientists in their own right. While encouraging them to take an independent stance on what they feel curious about, just make sure they don't hurt themselves doing something to satisfy their curiosity.

Another glimpse of their curious natures we get from how they insist on watching certain things playing out in action to see them with their own eyes. Like flushing the toilet repeatedly to simply watch the water rushing around the toilet bowl, or throwing a bowl down the stairs to see how it bounces off each stair. These and many such actions are a common sight for the parents of a toddler. Encourage and explain to satisfy their curiosity wherever possible. For other times, like the repeated toilet flushing, you can simply try to redirect them and divert their attention to more interesting things. Saying something entirely unrelated yet intriguing enough will help you handle your toddler in such situations. Like, "Do you know what mommy made for dinner today? Let's see if you can guess correctly," could be a good enough diversion.

Independent thinking and curious minds are bound to lead to the development of some truly remarkable personalities. Encourage your toddler to think and explore on their own to encourage good personality development.

Stop Saying Easy

Many times it so happens that we parents, in our infinite love for our children and to spare them trouble and possible heartache, tell them that what they are trying to do is easy, intending to tell them it's not difficult and should be a piece of cake for them. We say this as a means of encouragement for them to try different things. For example, if your child is wary of the oncoming exams, and you say, "It is nothing. I have faced tougher examinations in my age. You have it easy. Don't worry, you can do it." Though you say it as an encouragement, the only thing that your child has registered is that what is coming is an easy exam to what you have comparatively faced in your own childhood. Now, if they pass the exam, they have no real satisfaction because it was an easy one anyway. If they don't do well, then they have failed at something that was too easy, which then becomes embarrassing. For toddlers, imagine coaxing them into a tub of bath water that they are apprehensive about. You say, "It's alright, once you get in, it's easy."

If your child, at that instance, is unable to overcome the fear or apprehension and puts it off for some other time, then your child would feel embarrassed at having failed at something that was too easy and obvious.

Instead, make it something that's a little challenging. If they accomplish the thing, then they would have been successful at something hard, and if they failed, they would at least know that it was a tough thing anyway.

You could say something like, "I know it is a little hard. But I think you should give it a try. You could do it. Would you like to try?"

Toddlers are more receptive to this concept as they are too young to understand the emotional intricacies involved in such a scenario and would, therefore, be ideal to encourage into trying something they are scared or worried about.

Resources Outside Home

Children rely on parents for almost every need. For them, their parents are their world, their idea of what perfect looks like. They expect their parents to understand and know about everything. This is why they pose every question and every doubt to their parents, expecting them to know the answers to all their questions. Though this is good in its own way, it is also important to encourage kids to widen their resources. They could ask their doctor uncle about what causes diseases, what germ are like and so on. They could ask their grandparents where carrots grow while they tend to their garden. Under their parents' guidance they could be encouraged to explore their surroundings and learn from their observations. They visit the shopping mall, see the cashier generating bills off a machine, they watch a mailman or a courier service deliver a parcel, they visit a hospital and see the nurses and the doctors tending to their patients; all this and many more are opportunities for them to learn and grow. Their independent minds are bound to observe, absorb, and learn from what they see at such various places. It is important to encourage healthy and supervised exploration, especially for toddlers.

Toddlers can begin easily by interacting with the extended family first and then slowly move onto bigger and bolder resources. What this does is one, it teaches them how many things function and work around them and two, it prepares them for when they will eventually have to separate from their parents when going to school.

Children are known to experience separation anxiety when they are away from their parents. But it is a good idea that they are kept away from parents occasionally for limited amounts of time. This can also be achieved when parents take the time to give themselves a break and, in doing so, leave the kids in the care of a sitter or a relative. Though it will be a little difficult early on for them to understand why they have been separated from their parents and the comfort of the 'familiar', they will get used to it and will train themselves in coping with situations when they are away. They will learn that it is alright to trust others whom their parents seem to trust enough to leave them with. Children will learn to not be dependent upon their parents for their every need and will learn to look after and handle themselves when on their own. This will foster a sense of self-sufficiency and independence within children, which is an important trait to develop as they grow.

Let Children Dream

How many times have our children presented before us what we thought as the most absurd thing we had ever heard? "Mommy, how nice would it be if we could sit on a bird and fly around the world?" "If we could take a picnic basket and a blanket to the moon, and spend an evening there, wouldn't it be great, Daddy?"

Such statements are common from toddlers and also a little older kids who have just stepped into the world of imagination and dreaming. One very important thing to keep in mind is to realize that sharing this was a huge deal for your child. They are, in a way, trusting you with their most precious thoughts and expect validation of some kind. But, sadly, many parents respond with something like, "Don't be silly. That's not possible."

We simply brush these away as silly and unreal. Of course they are unreal and far fetched. But kids aren't truly interested in experiencing their dream as much as they are in simply dreaming it. They wish to share with you their imaginations to only be able to extrapolate it by expanding the whole 'what if' scenario. Instead, imagine if you respond with something like, "yeah, and we could take sandwiches and a bottle of juice. The moon would already be shining, so we probably wouldn't need any light." You would be encouraging their imaginations to grow and for them to think and realize what things are realistic and what are simply far fetched and dream-worthy. By contributing your own two cents to their 'what if' world, you are sharing a precious moment with them that they are bound to treasure. Imagine the good such a conversation could do to your relationship with your child. This could become a part of your own special time with each other. Doing this motivates children to think independently, and they will also be more open and less hesitant to share their thoughts and accomplishments with you. If you squash their imaginations without giving them your support and brush them off as silly, chances are, your child will withdraw themselves from you and become hesitant of sharing anything with you in the future. Encouraging them this way builds confidence in them and they become more trusting of you.

Teaching Responsibility

One important personality trait that it is never too early to develop or encourage in a child is responsibility. Raising responsible children is every parent's dream, and the earlier parents begin work on it, the more successful they will be. There are a few things parents can implement and incorporate in their children's schedules and routines to encourage responsibility.

Including Toddlers in Chores and Activities

When toddlers are made to feel as significant members of a household, they take their roles seriously. If you treat kids as insignificant and make them feel inadequate, it spurs them into misbehaviors and rebellions. Imagine a child who is included in the regular family meetings in a household, and asked to contribute in some way. Imagine the sense of importance and accomplishment this child would feel on being included as a useful member of the family. They can tell what they would contribute to the family's daily routine. Something simple like placing silverware on the table, keeping magazines in the rack, and so on, can become significant contributions from a toddler who might otherwise be pushed into the background. This is an effective way to teach kids responsibility from an early age. Make it a point to give them simple age-appropriate chores and encourage them when they do their bit. Irrespective of the quality of the job done, acknowledge their efforts and encourage them to keep trying. This will ensure that toddlers stick to their activities responsibly and take their roles and significance in the household seriously.

Encourage to Be Undemanding

When children are too dependent on their parents and expect every small thing from them, they become demanding and lack responsibility. To ensure your kids are not too dependent on you and are self-reliant, encourage them to be undemanding. Do not rush forward every time they need something of you that they can do by themselves with ease. Encourage them to do their own chores and not expect your help. When they need a glass of water, place glasses within their reach, teach them how to fill water, and the need to put the glass back at its place when they are finished. When they ask of you things that they are capable of doing, offer them choices and place limits. "Would you like me to show you how to sort the toys?" or "Would you like me to show you how to do it on your own?". This is a simple way to push them into acting on their own.

Trust Your Kids

When you expect your children to act responsibly, they need you to trust them in return. You want your child to place the silverware on the table when you are setting the table for dinner, but you don't trust them enough to do a good job of it on their own. So you interrupt them mid-chore, correct them when they do something wrong, and so on. There is nothing wrong with teaching your child the right way to do a job, but how and when you do, it is important. If you never let your child finish a job and are always taking over mid-chore, then they would never get to finish the job and show you how they did. In the end, by not trusting them enough, you are not inspiring a sense of responsibility in them. If you can control yourself for a little while and hold your corrections until the job is done, let the child finish placing the silverware, encourage and praise their efforts and then offer your corrections, this would be more fruitful.

Handling Fears and Fights

One big parenting challenge that parents face all the time with kids of all ages, and more so with toddlers, is soothing their fears and handling their fights with other kids. Different parents react to these concerns differently, but only a positive parenting approach can ensure that your child becomes self-reliant in handling their own fears and taking care of themselves during fights. All other parenting approaches present temporary solutions that do not truly solve the situation, nor do they help the child in any way.

Fears - Yours and Theirs

Many children are afraid of the unknown. It is remarkable to know that children below two years of age are hardly afraid of anything other than perhaps getting separated from their mother. But as they grow, see and observe the world around them, hear other children and their siblings talk, hear stories, and watch TV, they grow and build these fears. Fear of the dark, fear of unknown monsters, fear of being alone, fear of insects or dogs, and so on, then become a common enough phenomenon for most toddlers.

Most parents, when presented with these fears, either would brush the fear off as silly or would try and be overprotective and 'over-soothe' their fears. A parent might respond saying, "There are no monsters, don't be silly" or maybe, "Don't worry, you can sleep with mommy tonight." But neither of these responses will help your child manage their fear. Because the fear *for them* isn't silly and it is bound to strike again tomorrow night. Simply brushing it off doesn't work and your child will not be reassured. Instead, because you could not address their fears and validate their feelings, they lose their trust in you. It will be harder for them to come to you the next time they have an issue. Also, letting your child sleep with you because they're scared doesn't solve the issue. Instead, it is like telling them your fears are true, there might be a monster lurking somewhere. You also make your child dependent upon you for dealing with their fears and they never learn to overcome them.

What can you do instead to help your child with their fears? Try and work with your child to look for solutions to their fears. Discuss what would help them counter their fears. Would having a small light bulb, a candle, or a flashlight help them? Would looking for monsters under the bed with them using a flashlight assure them that none exist? Would a soothing music record help them sleep? Would using an anti-monsters spray (simply a spray bottle filled with water) help them stay courageous? Likewise, look for solutions for all of their fears. Validate their feelings of fear and help them realize that you understand them and are there to support them when they need you. Sharing your own fears that you had as a child and how you overcame them might help them overcome theirs. It is not necessary that they will have the same fears as you, and you must not expect them to. But knowing that such fears are normal and people have them and gradually overcome them is soothing for a child.

A lot of times, parents are the ones too scared about the well being of their kids. This is, at times, so extreme that parents become overprotective in trying to shield their kids from any harm. Fear of children meeting an accident, getting kidnapped, getting hurt or injured while playing are just some of the fears such overprotective parents experience.

But, just because we are scared, we cannot stifle our child's growth or movement. Would you rather have your child locked in their room for the fear of them getting hurt if they got out and played? Instead, try and equip them with means to take care of themselves as far as they can when something of this sort happens. For toddlers, encourage them to learn your phone numbers, and explain what simple first-aid is. Instruct them to come to you when something happens. For children up to the age of four to five years old, always have an adult oversee them as they play. But do not, for any reason, let your fears stop their natural growth and development. Children who have overprotective parents might go on to have several different kinds of phobias. One way to counter your own fears and let your children experience the world is to allow them to do what they are comfortable doing. Stand back and watch without interfering until they need you. If your three- or four-year-old wishes to learn to ride a bicycle, do not stop them. Instead, if you can't teach them, have your partner or spouse teach them to ride and you simply watch from a distance. Become active cheerleaders for them and encourage them as they try. It might so happen that you are scared of a thing that they really want to try. A mother was terrified of the joy rides in the amusement park, while her toddler was excited to experience sitting in a child roller coaster for the first time. Instead of transferring her own fears to the child, the mother encouraged her child and clapped as her child completed the ride. This is the attitude you need to have around your toddlers so they are not handicapped by their fears as they grow.

Sharing and Fights

This is another big issue that parents struggle with when it comes to toddlers. The resistance to share their belongings and fights between siblings or with other kids is a common cause of headache for parents. What we need to understand first is for kids who are two years old or younger, sharing doesn't come naturally, and it would be unfair to expect of them. They are entirely new to the concept of belongings being shareable.

For older kids of up to four years old, you will need to gently guide them on how to share things. You could try sharing something of yours and tell them so. "This is mine, but I would like to share this with you." When you do this, ensure that your kids know that they have a responsibility toward the shared item and must return it as is after using it. This helps them understand that sharing is good and they will model their behavior after you. Make sure to have more than one shareable item for your kids so that when one is shared with a friend or sibling, they still have something else to hold onto for themselves. Sharing is an acquired skill. Kids are not inclined to share inherently but they can be taught to share as they grow. Encourage and appreciate them when they share their belongings. Do not name call or lecture them when they do not share. Instead, validate their feelings and see how you can help them.

Also, it is important to understand that the toddler age is fickle. They would share once and refuse to share at another time. This is completely normal. Simply keep working with your child in a positive manner. Let them sort things into two groups; one that they are willing to share, and another that is exclusively for them. Doing this will assure them that they will only have to share a part of their belongings and not all of them. This will encourage them to part with things more readily. Holding onto a few select belongings that are special will make them feel secure and give them a sense of independence and privacy. Let them understand that they mustn't touch others' private and personal things similarly. Make it a point to discuss in your family meetings how one should respect others' belongings, not taking them without permission and returning them intact and on time. Read to them stories that involve sharing. Take them to a library to understand the concept of sharing and borrowing. Remind them repeatedly that it is healthy to share.

Fights are a huge and regular problem in households with more than one child. Apart from fights with one's siblings, children also seem to engage in fights with visiting kids or kids at the park and so on. This can become a nuisance for parents if not addressed correctly and promptly. Simply shouting and yelling won't do the trick. A positive approach is needed to counter such situations. Many parents resort to taking sides in a fight either with one of the siblings or with their own child when the fight is with children from other families. This is damaging to the child at many levels. Taking sides tells the child that what they were involved in was right and has the parent's stamp of approval. It gives them a license to repeat the behavior again and again. How many times have we noticed that when adults or neighbors fight over their children, the kids would have long forgotten that something like a fight did happen?

When your toddlers are involved in fights, do not take sides or get in the middle of it, trying to find the cause and diffuse the situation. This will be a temporary solution. Instead, if the fight is silly and does not involve serious hitting, simply sit quietly around your children as they fight it off. After a couple of back and forths, your children are bound to go on and forget it. When they involve you themselves, instead of taking sides, encourage them to work it out amongst themselves. If the fighting is over a toy, you can simply pick the toy and keep it in a place that neither can get to. Then tell them, "You can have it back when you have resolved your fight and can work on how you are going to share it between yourselves." You can talk to them about your own fights in your childhood and how you handled those. Encourage your children to be compassionate with their siblings. Do this not when they are fighting but rather when they are calm. You could even make this a part of your problem-solving family meeting topic for a day and invite kids to present possible solutions to fighting. You will be amazed to see how well kids respond and how many different solutions they can come up with when asked for their input. Chalk out prearranged agreements when your family limits are broken with respect to fighting. Tell them inspiring stories or read to them books as a part of your special time together that show the negative effects of fighting. Use positive time-outs or a visit to their quiet place to help them calm down. Let them try talking with their siblings once again, when they are in control of their emotions. One thing to keep in mind, though, is fights are inevitable and will inadvertently happen at one time or the other. Your job as a parent is to ensure your children stay safe and do not cause each other serious injury. Otherwise, it would be wise to step back and allow your children to work toward a solution themselves by only guiding them wherever necessary.

CHAPTER 9:

TAKING CARE OF YOURSELF

Parenting in itself is a tough job. Parenting toddlers is super tough. While you struggle to handle that little bundle of energy, oftentimes you forget about yourself. We are so invested in the well-being and care of our little one that our own health and mental sanity take a back seat.

Toddlers are energy driven curious beings. With their curious nature and ever-developing emotional repertoire, they unwittingly throw many challenges before us. Understandably, such challenging behaviors can strain our patience to breaking point and frustrate us to no end. It becomes, therefore, even more important that you take a breather every now and then so you do not lose your own balance and control of emotions. Remember that if you lose control of your emotions and get exceptionally angry over your child, not because they have done something so unpardonable, but because you are so frustrated with continued stress of misbehavior that a point comes where your patience breaks, you will only harm your child more. As innocent as toddlers are, they are incapable of doing something unpardonable that would deserve or justify the use of force on your part. It is important, therefore, to act before the situation reaches that boiling point, that threshold where things could tip over for worse.

Controlled Reactions

The best step that you can take as a parent is to take care of your own emotions in a timely manner. If you are working hard and struggling to teach your child emotional control and addressing challenging behaviors, it all comes to nothing if you yourself end up losing control of your emotions.

Many times, we as parents are tempted to simply shout, slap, or yell at our children. But, if you wish to be a positive parent, take care that your actions or reactions to your child are hasty and rushed. Make it a point to breathe deeply (remember the breathing exercises!) and calm yourself before addressing your child. Count at least up to ten to give yourself time to calm your mind and swallow that frustration and anger. This is an important step to practice before you talk to your child after a difficult situation or as a reaction to their misbehavior. Imagine what you could do to your child if you did not calm yourself and take the time to think clearly and with positivity before approaching them. Keeping this thought and this realization always at the forefront of your being as a parent will help you reign in your emotions and not act rashly.

Self-Care

Beyond providing consistent and controlled reactions each time to every misbehavior, it is important to make your own self-care a priority. Allot time for taking care of yourself each day. But what exactly is self-care? It is like filling up your tank before you begin each day fresh and rejuvenated. It is giving your mind and body the rest it deserves. It is to give yourself the ability to handle your own social and emotional needs as an individual and not just as a parent. Self-care might is the last thing on your mind now when all your focus is on your toddler and giving them your best. But, you can't really give them your best when you are not your hundred percent self. Think of the safety instructions on flights. They always say that if pressure in the cabin drops, you must put on your oxygen mask first before assisting your child. Of course, our initial instinct is first to take care of our child. But, if we do not get oxygen, we may pass out and will not be able to take care of our child or ourselves. The same goes for life. We must have our needs met so that we can care for our family properly. There are a few things that you can do to give yourself proper care. Plan to experiment with the different self-care strategies so you are able to decide what strategies work best for you.

Meditation

A short and quick meditation spell can help you feel refreshed. If you are new to the world of meditation, there are several resources available to guide you through various meditation techniques. Make a habit of meditating for at least five minutes every day, either in the morning or in the evening, so that you remain calm and rejuvenated every day. You can even include your child in your daily meditational episodes so that you both can benefit greatly from this important life skill. I have included a special meditation bonus session for you at the end of this book.

Spending Time Outdoors

An excellent idea is to spend sufficient time outdoors near nature. It has been observed that simply watching greenery for a certain period of time has a very soothing effect on the mind. Therefore, if you could squeeze time out to spend at least a little time per week at a place full of greenery, close to nature and its elements, it would be greatly calming and rejuvenating for you. Look for hillsides, riverbanks, mountain treks, waterfall resorts, or any such spots that you can easily reach for a quick refreshing trip. If once in a week is not workable for you, you could opt for other self-care techniques and keep outdoors to a minimum of once in a month or two.

Music

This is one of the easiest ways to stay calm and poised. Simply listen to any music that you like, which you are confident would calm you. You could listen to music at almost any time. Whether you are feeling stressed or not, you can simply tune into your favorite music as you go about your daily chores around the house. An advantage of using music to stay calm is there is no real need to set aside time to listen to soothing music. It can be done while you are busy with other work too.

Book Clubs

Another good way to keep motivated and stay positive is to join a book club. Joining a book club can help you in many ways. A club that meets in person will give you opportunities to have regular social connections. It will provide you with constant motivation to set aside time for regular reading sessions. You will be with like-minded people once every week, which will help keep your emotions grounded. Book clubs will be more helpful when they include in-person meetings and are not just online interactions. Usually, online book clubs have a really large number of members, which can make them impersonal and, as a result, will not be as motivating as face-to-face meetings and goal settings can be.

Physical Exercise

Keeping physically active apart from all the work you do around the house will greatly help you stay fit and refreshed. A time and activity assigned explicitly for the purpose of exercise will work positively on your mindset. If you are unable to hit the gym for some reason, simply taking a walk outdoors for at least fifteen minutes will do wonders for your positive approach to daily issues.

Maintain a Journal

If you are able to write your thoughts and feelings regularly in a diary or a journal, it would be greatly beneficial in relaxing you and emptying your mind of stressful thoughts and problematic issues. This can be a great tool to keep you positive and feeling good about your life. When things become tough, you can make it a point to just write down at least three things you are happy about and grateful for. This can become your own gratitude journaling exercise. It will help you retain a positive outlook on life and avoid feelings of excessive frustrations and annoyance.

Pamper Yourself

You could take time out to treat yourself with a few simple pleasures. These need not necessarily be luxuries. Simple things like an aromatic massage, a hot bath, some soothing music, lighting scented candles around the house, or drinking rejuvenating herbal teas can all be great ways to pamper yourself and give yourself some much-needed attention.

Spend Time With Family and Friends

If you can make time to get away from the busy schedules and the hustle and bustle of daily life to spend time with your friends, it would be a great way to unwind. Get some away time from kids by having someone watch over them while you take a much-needed breather. This will help you relax, and you will be able to get back in the groove after the retreat with more vigor and energy.

Get Away From Gadgets

Though it is usually assumed that watching something on your mobile or the television will help you relax, and it is true to some extent, oftentimes it is the contrary that is true. From one social app to another, you can simply feel stressed into replying to messages, emails, and whatnot. Instead, if you can spare time for a digital detox, it will be extremely beneficial for you.

Take Care of Basics

Getting out once in a while with your spouse or friends for lunch or a dinner date can be a good idea to relax. You could even go on a long drive on your own to unwind yourself. But all these excellent ideas will be for nothing if you are not attentive toward the most basic needs of your body. These are to eat a healthy diet and get sufficient sleep of at least seven to eight hours a day, along with minimum physical exercise. If these basics aren't met, your body would feel the strain most excessively, and any number of extra calming and relaxing techniques would be useless.

Another important factor is to watch your water intake. Hydration plays a vital role in how your body handles different situations. Insufficient water intake can make you tired with lower energy levels. Stress has been found to be directly related to water intake. The more you drink water, the better your body is able to handle stress toxins and flush them out regularly. Taking small sips of water regularly every ten to fifteen minutes has been found to help relax your stress centers in the brain. After all, our body is 70% water, while our brain alone is 85% water. This is why when we are stressed and are not drinking enough water, as usually happens, we feel mild to severe headaches and neck aches. Counter all this by simply making it a point to be well hydrated at all times. If you do not normally drink water, try to increase your intake of healthy fluids like juices or herbal teas. Try carrying a small bottle of water around with you as you go outside or even as you do chores. Many times, the simple task of fetching ourselves a glass of water seems like a mountain to climb when we are tired and we put it off for later. Avoid this by having a water bottle handy for regular sips to stay fresh. You will see a remarkable difference in how you are able to cope with stress just by being well hydrated.

It is vital that you give yourself regular doses of much-needed self-care. With the help of these few strategies, you will be able to handle most of the stressful situations that arise in your life as a parent. But when things are too tough for you to handle, and no calming technique or relaxing strategy seems to work and you truly feel yourself breaking under the strain of it all, opt for professional help. There is nothing wrong or shameful about going to a therapist or counselor who can talk you through your troubles and help you navigate these difficult times. Just make sure that the person you visit is a certified and licensed professional and you are confident of their ability to help you.

The bottom line is not to let your well-being, your emotional and physical health take a back seat amidst all the parenting strain. Remember, each phase is bound to pass. Only when you are healthy and motivated can you give your child your best.

CONCLUSION

In this book, we have seen how difficult parenting toddlers can be. We have seen the best way to approach the positive parenting methodology. We have seen in detail what are the expected appropriate behaviors for this age and the different challenging behaviors that toddlers seem to surprise us with constantly.

We have seen a positive way to handle these challenging behaviors. From introducing safe and quiet places for your child to having routines, schedules, reward charts and feeling charts, we have seen some concrete actionables that can help you implement the positive parenting methodology.

We have also seen how important forming a connection can be as well as how destructive it can be for a child to feel disconnected and unloved. Several challenging behaviors stem from the fact that the child needs to feel connected and loved. It is unfortunate, truly, how our present-day education systems around the world have stifled the need of kids to feel a bond around them, and it has all become a rat race of who does better than the next person. In all this mayhem, we have forgotten that a child as young as a toddler would not need instructive criticism, which is amply available, but rather a loving and empathetic adult presence around them, which is too rare to find. Kids as young as three are seen to become deflectors and defensive blamers. Who is to blame? As ironic as this question seems, it is us parents, the first interactors kids come to know, that are responsible for this growing disregard for a child's emotions and feelings.

Toddlers, with their innocence and ever-growing emotional and mental maturity, are constantly presenting us with challenges. Their need to be curious and inquisitive explorers adds to our parenting challenges in its own way. They are like little balls of energy that are too full of unspent zeal, which need constant instruction and direction to grow and mature to their full potential. They are still too fragile and directionless to stand on their own. Their developmental needs require that their emotional literacy be satisfied timely and with ease. Positive parenting accomplishes this without undue force or punishments. Empathy is a huge pillar of this parenting technique and we have seen how helpful being empathetic can be, both for your child and for you. Unlike traditional parenting, positive parenting lets you take care and groom your child with the least amount of stress for the both of you. The focus here is on being positive and empathetic in any given situation, without giving space to negativity and punishments.

We, as parents, must understand that what we intend to do is to give our children the necessary skills that will help them regulate their emotions and problem solve on their own when they face an issue. We do not want to dictate to them actions and their consequences every step of the way. Our goal through positive discipline is to ensure that the child feels safe in their environment, amongst family and friends, and is able to connect with their own emotions and understand their actions and the impact they have on others.

We parents are in a state of power over our children. We are the authority they look up to. They come to us for their issues and problem solving. What we are required to do is identify the conflicts our children face and present them with solutions. As much as we would like to hold on to our positions of authority in the household, as we rightly should, we forget that this position of power does not give us leave to be a bully or tyrant in our own homes. Though many parents who follow traditional parenting methods are extremely loving and would simply blanch out of their skins if called tyrants in their homes, unwittingly so, we are being just that. We abuse our power as parents to reduce eager innocent toddlers to machines that simply work to please us. Would you want your child to behave nicely because they are scared of you, and they wish to please you, or would you rather they behave admirably because they have truly understood what you were trying to teach them? That is exactly the difference positive parenting brings to the 'parenting' table. But, positive parenting goes a little deeper than this. Through positive parenting, you are not just giving solutions, but rather you are being non-judgmental and giving solutions that actually last a lifetime because your focus is to encourage the development of skills rather than provide quick fixes. We can do this only when we have the necessary skills ourselves. This is where the importance of regulating that 'power' a parent has stems from. A positive parent, having a positive intention, will act with composure, encouragement, firmness, giving appropriate choices, and would be extremely empathetic. What would you term as a positive intention? When parents respond to behaviors with the intention of encouraging the child toward good behavior and positive change would be a positive intention.

This will never happen in a day. This is a lengthy, time-consuming process that is bound to take time, effort, and a considerable amount of patience on your part. But, as you keep at it, you will be amazed to see the results following a few simple strategies has led you to. It will take practice both on your part as well as your child's, but you will succeed with the help of using effective parenting strategies in the end. There are bound to be times when you feel overwhelmed, but remind yourself of your intention, the bigger goal in the end of having a child with admirable personality traits, and your discomfort and frustrations are bound to disappear as you internalize this thought. As we saw earlier in this book, the base of all good parenting stems from having the right attitude toward the actions of your child, keeping the whole parenting methodology positive and motivational. The key here is to realize that in the end, as a parent, you would not want to punish your child, you would rather teach them!

I'D LOVE YOUR HELP

As a self-publishing author, reviews are the lifeblood of my work.

I would be over-the-moon thankful if you could take just 60 seconds to leave a brief review on Amazon.

I know you must be busy and I truly appreciate your time, even a few short sentences would be greatly helpful.

Don't forget to get your complimentary

GAMES AND ACTIVITIES
FOR POSITIVE DISCIPLINE

Here's what you'll learn from this bonus:

- My top 7 games and activities to teach your child about discipline the positive parenting way
- How to craft the tools for the games at home
- Why it is so important to teach your kids to play and learn at the same time

Toddler discipline, and well, life in general, is much easier when everyone in the house is having some fun!

Get your 7 games and activities right here:

http://gracestockholm.net/toddler-discipline-fun-games/

BONUS SECTION: GUIDED MEDITATION FOR PARENTS AND KIDS

In this bonus section, I have prepared 2 special guided meditation sessions, 45 minutes each.

The first is for you, the parent. Meditating is a great way to relieve stress and keep composure throughout our hectic lives. In this meditation, we will focus on the connection with our inner child which will enable you to better understand and cope with your child, even in challenging times and situations.

The second session is for your child. In this session your child will learn the benefits of meditating as well as be more empowered and focused. You will probably want to sit with your child for this session, at least for the first few times. If you have a younger child and the session is too long for them, simply do a few minutes at a time and gradually increase the meditation time.

If this is the audio version, just dive in.

If this is the kindle or paperback version, sit down and read it to yourself slowly.

Session #1 - For You

-I am so excited that you are about to embark on this meditation session for us, the parents. This practice will be about one hour long. Our main focus today will be positive parenting, the most important and rewarding way in which you can raise your children.

-Before diving into meditation today, what I want you to do first is to find a place where you can comfortably sit for the next 50 to 60 minutes. This is a longer session, which means staying comfortable in one place is crucial. You can sit on the floor, on a mattress, or directly on the ground. Or you can sit on the couch, or on a very comfortable chair.

-Just find your most relaxed pose as you set yourself into the meditation spot. You don't have to sit in a lotus position for the practice, although if it feels comfortable for you definitely give that a go. You can sit whichever way you want as long as you're comfortable.

-Whenever you're ready, we'll go ahead and start the meditation with a simple breathing exercise. What you need to do is to simply breathe in through the nose, and then exhale through the mouth. Do it loud enough so that people in the other room could hear you.

-Continue to breathe like this for a few moments now. Simply focus on the expansion of your chest as the air goes in, and then at the contraction of the rib cage as it goes out. Focus on the area of the chest where the breathing takes place. And as you breathe out one last time, gently close the eyes.

-And as you close your eyes, leave the breathing out of focus for a second. It will allow it to go back to its natural state, in and out through the nose.

-Without leaving the breath out of focus anywhere on the course of this practice today, we'll begin to regroup to our bodies by simply sensing the level of weight it brings down upon the chair or the floor that we're on.

-We are also focusing on where the legs and the arms are touching the floor beneath us or the lap, depending on where you've sat. There's nothing to be done here, just feeling the weight of the different parts of the body as we connect the mind with the physical.

-You are doing great. Remember to always keep a gentle focus on the act of breathing. Do not lose focus on the expansion and contraction of your chest, as this simple noticing will keep you grounded for the rest of the practice.

-The focus of today's meditation is the word "positivity" and everything that it represents. Being positive starts with acting positive, even if the situation might not always be positive. For example, whenever you're trying to teach your child a lesson, after he or she got into trouble, some of us naturally think about the negative aspect to say.

-Acting positive is important here because it leads the way from an almost certain conflict to a positive experience for you and your child. This will help the young one understand the power of staying and acting positive in the future.

-Positivity is at the core of everything that is good. Think positively and you'll behave positively. Act positively and you'll be treated the same way by the people around you. For this idea of positive parenting, we'll be focusing on a technique meant to bring a better understanding of positivity into our daily lives.

-Before moving into the next part of the session today, I want you to once again regroup your focus on your breathing. And just for a moment now, stay with your breath the entire time. From the moment you inhale and feel the air going through the nose, the air canals and into the lungs, all the way through the mouth, until the air leaves the system.

-We will now move on to the visualization part of our practice today. Visualization is an incredibly powerful meditation technique. It allows us to go through the depths of the mind, visualizing situations, things, ideas and mechanisms that will help us through our days and make us realize how important it is to have a connected mind and body and how we can use the two for an enhanced version of ourselves.

-Visualization works by you enhancing not only your thoughts but also your feelings and emotions. It means you see an event in the mind but also feel and have a sense of it without being in the actual situation.

-Imagine you are cleaning the living room. You are dusting off the bookshelves, the TV and then moving on with sweeping the floor and vacuuming the rug. There, on the rug, there's a huge brown stain. You quickly realize it is melted chocolate, a great deal of it. You know who's responsible for it before even looking into the garbage bin for the package.

-What are your feelings right now as you stare at the big spot of melted chocolate on your favorite rug? Is it anger? Is it despair? Is it disappointment? What is it that you feel?

-Besides the feelings that you feel, which are the bodily sensations that the thoughts and emotions are bringing up right now? Do you feel any tremble in the body? Is your heart racing? Are there any sensations of sweat, of tingling, pulsating in the body?

-While all these sensations are normal when you are dealing with a negative situation, the goal we are going for today is to find the positive from all the issues that we're facing here. So, for a moment now, I want you to relax and focus on the breathing while still visualizing the pool of melted chocolate on the floor.

-Now I want you to shift the negative aspects of the situation for the positive ones. What makes this situation a positive one? I know it's hard to find a few reasons why a dirty spot on your rug is a positive thing, but just try to do so.

-For example, you can think about how happy your child was when he or she was enjoying the chocolate. And what they've gone through when accidently dropping the chocolate on the rug. How scared they were of the consequences, when in fact all that they did is not even close to being something that bad in the end.

-Great! Take a deep breath in through the nose, and then out through the mouth. We will now move to the second part of the visualization.

-Imagine you are in the supermarket with your toddler. You are walking through the store, buying this and that, whatever it is that you need. All of a sudden, your toddler starts screaming and shouting that they want candy. This candy is not on your shopping list that you've discussed at home.

-What are your feelings right now as you stare at the toddler screaming about the unapproved candy? Is it anger? Is it despair? Is it disappointment? What is it that you feel?

-Besides the feelings that you feel, what are the bodily sensations that the thoughts and emotions are bringing up right now? Do you feel any tremble in the body? Is your heart racing? Are there any sensations of sweat, of tingling, pulsating in the body?

-Once again, while all these sensations are normal when you are dealing with a challenging situation, the goal we are going for today is to find the positive from all the issues that we're facing here. So for a moment now, I want you to relax and focus on the breathing while still visualizing the kid running around the store angrily.

-Now I want you to shift the negative aspects of the situation to the positive ones. What makes this situation a positive one? I know it's hard to find a few reasons why your child screaming in a public space is a positive thing, but just try to do so.

-For example, you can think of it as a teaching moment for your child about delaying gratifications and keeping their word. You can teach your child about healthy substitutes and work together with them to find a snack that is both desirable and nutritious. You can also just be there for your child, contain him or her and show them that they will be loved even if they scream their heads off in a public place.

-Just try to find one or two more positive aspects of the situation as you breathe in gently through the nose, and then out through the mouth.

-Finally, we will move to the last part of the visualization, the last challenging situation for today.

-Imagine you are trying to put your toddler to sleep. You just put on their pajamas and are tucking them into bed. The moment you try to do this though, they start resisting and demanding some more TV and a snack. You try to make them understand it is now bedtime, but they don't take "no" for an answer and frantically scream, waking up your newborn in the other room.

-What is it that you are feeling right now, as you witness your toddler refusing to go to bed after a long day and screaming around? Is it anger? Is it despair? Is it disappointment? What is it that you feel?

-Besides the feelings that you feel, what are the bodily sensations that the thoughts and emotions are bringing up right now? Do you feel any tremble in the body? Is your heart racing? Are there any sensations of sweat, of tingling, pulsating in the body?

-While as we know that all these sensations are normal when you are dealing with a challenging situation, the goal we are going for today is to find the positive from all the scenarios that we're facing here. So for a second now, I want you to relax and again focus on the breathing while still visualizing your toddler screaming in their bed and you now awake newborn screaming in the next room.

-Now I want you to shift the negative aspects of the situation for the positive ones. What makes this situation a positive one? It isn't easy to find a few reasons why your toddler refusing to go to sleep is a positive thing, but just try to do so.

-You can think about the joy and relaxation on your toddler's face when they finally go to sleep. Even if they are now refusing to do so, you know that they are so tired and cranky, which is possibly the reason why they refuse to go to bed and throw a fit. In reality, all that they actually want is to actually sleep. You just need to stick with it and they will relax and sleep like a baby in just a few moments.

-You have done great with this visualization practice today. Really well. Take a moment to relax, sit back, maybe regroup the body which has been standing still for a while now. Let's also focus on the breath. Take a few gentle breaths in and out through the nose, as you relax the body.

-Following the visualization practice, we will move into the next part of this meditation today. With this part, we will be focusing on a series of positive affirmations that will help you better cope with the challenges of toddler discipline and reinforce the ideas about positive parenting that you're already familiar with from the book.

-We'll begin by reading each affirmation twice, then have a small "chat", so to say, about each of them. I'll guide you all throughout the entire thing, so no worries there. Let's begin.

-For this first affirmation, I want you to slowly bring your awareness to the sound of my voice as well as to your breath. Here's the first one, so listen very carefully.

-There is no one better to be than myself. I am great. And I get better every single day by keeping myself positive.

-There is no one better to be than myself. I am great. And I get better every single day by keeping myself positive.

<<PAUSE FOR 10 SECONDS>>

-Great job. When people are losing it, they're usually doing it because they can't see the good in the bad. Keeping a positive attitude towards anything that you do in life is essential for facing any challenging issue.

-The second affirmation is now ready for us to listen to. Again, take a few breaths and become completely aware of your mind and body. Here we go with this next one right now.

-I am an amazing person because I can find solutions to all of my problems. This makes me a better person and a leader every day.

-I am an amazing person because I can find solutions to all of my problems. This makes me a better person and a leader every day.

<<PAUSE FOR 10 SECONDS>>

-Good! The most amazing person that you can be is you and only you. And great people solve problems regardless of how challenging they might be. Leaders are becoming better and better because of it with each day that passes.

-Here comes the third affirmation for our practice today. The rule is simple now, simply listen to this affirmation and keep a gentle concentration on your breathing. This will help you better understand and incorporate the powerful affirmation into your deep mind.

-I forgive myself for my mistakes. My mistakes are my challenges. And my challenges help me grow because I learn from every single one of them.

-I forgive myself for my mistakes. My mistakes are my challenges. And my challenges help me grow because I learn from every single one of them.

<<PAUSE FOR 10 SECONDS>>

-Very good! Mistakes are a normal part of one's life. You cannot leave without making mistakes. They're the most powerful source of self-help and learning you can have. Mistakes can be terrible, yet if we extract the knowledge from them, they turn into blessings.

-We are now about to listen to our fourth affirmation today. Take a moment to regroup and listen to your breathing, then get ready by focusing your attention to your sense of hearing. Here we go.

-Right now, I am perfect just the way I am. I am a good person and I am always up for becoming better while being forgiving towards myself.

-Right now, I am perfect just the way I am. I am a good person and I am always up for becoming better while being forgiving towards myself.

<<PAUSE FOR 10 SECONDS>>

-You're doing great. Sometimes people do not value themselves for who they are. They can roam around always waiting for someone to tell them how great they are. Do it yourself! You are amazing, you are powerful, you are outstanding, just the way you are!

-We have one more affirmation before taking a little break in our practice today. Here's our affirmation number five for you. Listen carefully.

-Today is going to be an amazing day. I have the confidence and the courage to tackle whatever life will throw at me in the following hours. I am determined to do great things.

-Today is going to be an amazing day. I have the confidence and the courage to tackle whatever life will throw at me in the following hours. I am determined to do great things.

<<PAUSE FOR 10 SECONDS>>

-Nice, you're doing very good so far. Setting your daily goal towards having a great day is the ideal way to go for any of your activities. Confidence is key, courage is the motor that's driving it, and positivity is the overall sense that you have to have in order to follow through.

-As we're now in the middle of our affirmations practice, we'll be taking a short break from them. Just try to focus on the gentle breath that has now started to slow down naturally, without you even having to think about it.

-Follow a few of these breaths now, as the air goes into the nose and the lungs, and then moves out the same way. Easily concentrate your attention on this process.

-And as you do so, remember to keep a positive attitude not just towards yourself but also towards this very meditation practice that you're doing right now. It's very important to recognize its benefits now and for the foreseeable future.

-We have now reached the sixth affirmation of our session today. Take a few seconds to gently focus on the breathing again, as well as on the words you're about to listen to.

-I control my own happiness. I am responsible for it, I can create and I can let it go. This makes me completely responsible for how I feel.

-I control my own happiness. I am responsible for it, I can create and I can let it go. This makes me completely responsible for how I feel.

<<PAUSE FOR 10 SECONDS>>

-Good one. It's a known fact that whatever happens to us in life, we are the ones who decide on whether to be miserable or happy about it. This is a huge responsibility for us all, which is why so many people simply fail to turn themselves into happy beings. Being and staying happy is something you have to actively do, consciously reach for every single moment of your life.

-Here we are now at our seventh affirmation. Again, listen to it carefully, both times it's going to be read to you, while keeping yourself focused on the breath.

-I have people in my life who love me and care for me just the way I am. I have true friends who will always be there for me when I need them, unconditionally.

-I have people in my life who love me and care for me just the way I am. I have true friends who will always be there for me when I need them, unconditionally.

<<PAUSE FOR 10 SECONDS>>

-Nice. The people you're surrounding yourself with are reflecting the exact person you are. If you're around good positive people, there is no chance you're going to ever turn into something other than that. The contrary applies as well. True friends will tell you the truth in your face, while supporting you.

-We are eight affirmations in with this next one. This practice might be a tad challenging for some, but think about the benefits of it. And keep yourself positive. Let's listen to the next one.

126

-I stand up for what I believe in. I believe in myself, in my goals, my dreams, and the people around me. I will not let myself stop believing in the good in life.

-I stand up for what I believe in. I believe in myself, in my goals, my dreams, and the people around me. I will not let myself stop believing in the good in life.

<<PAUSE FOR 10 SECONDS>>

-Very good one. Believing in everything that you are dreaming for in life starts with believing in yourself. If that central aspect is missing from your thinking and your way of being, you're not fully ready to actually accomplish what you want in life. It all starts with a simple belief. I believe in myself. That's all that you need to do.

-Here's the ninth affirmation of this series now. Gently focus on the breath for a few moments before we move along and listen to it. Alright, let's go.

-It's okay not knowing everything in life. I am constantly learning about life, work, personal affairs, relationships, myself. If there's room for learning, and there's always room for that, there's room for growth and life.

-It's okay not knowing everything in life. I am constantly learning about life, work, personal affairs, relationships, myself. If there's room for learning, and there's always room for that, there's room for growth and life.

<<PAUSE FOR 10 SECONDS>>

-Nice! Not knowing everything is part of being human. Actually, that is a fact. No one knows everything. But acknowledging that we do not know is where growth happens. Learning is proof we are alive and well.

-Well, here we are at the final affirmation, number ten. As with the last nine, gently focus on the words you're about to hear.

-I can get through anything. I can do whatever I put my mind to. When I fall, I get up and do it again - better, stronger, and more confident than the last time. I never fail. Failure only occurs if I stop trying.

-I can get through anything. I can do whatever I put my mind to. When I fall, I get up and do it again - better, stronger, and more confident than the last time. I never fail. Failure only occurs if I stop trying.

<<PAUSE FOR 10 SECONDS>>

-Awesome job! I want you to remember in life to get up and try again, whenever things did not go your way. Not succeeding is not defeat. Not succeeding is just another proof that you've not given up. Do it again and again, stay positive and be ready for new and new tries.

-We are now getting close to the end of our meditation session today. As we're approaching the final steps, we're going to be focusing on our emotions, thoughts and feelings by performing a quick mind scan. This mind scan is designed to help you better listen to the mind. We don't control the thoughts or dreams of the mind. What we can control are our actions that we take, in the mind, when it throws unwanted thoughts and feelings towards us.

-We will leave the body for now and focus on the mind, the place where the emotions, thoughts and feelings are coming from. The epicenter of all that is representing ourselves. Here's where everything, every aspect of our lives, happen.

-First, I want you to scan your mind for whatever thoughts are running in it at this very moment. What is the mind thinking about? What are the thoughts about? Are these thoughts helpful in any way? Or are there just thoughts that create some tension or trouble in the mind?

-Second, we will be focusing on the emotions these thoughts are producing right now. Do you have any dominant emotion that is present at this moment in the mind? Is there any happiness, calm, relaxation? Are there any tendencies for sadness, anger or irritation?

-Third and finally, we'll be focusing on the feelings that the body is feeling right now. See if there are any feelings that you feel in your body. Whatever they might be, you only have to notice them and by not judging any of them, thoughts, emotions and feelings, see them go away.

-Focus on the breathing right now, as we're getting ready to come back to the moment of now. Take a few big, deep breaths in through the nose, and then release the air out through the mouth. Feel the sensation of touch between the body and whatever it is that you are sitting on. The sounds around you, the different smells and even tastes in the mouth.

-And with this final exhale, gently open the eyes. Remember to keep the feeling of positivity all throughout the day today and apply it to whatever it is that you're doing. Wherever you go, stay positive and well. Whatever you do, keep that sense of positivity into your life. Spread the sense of wellbeing around to others just like you, who might have a good or not so good day. Show them the power of staying positive, and they will face whatever they have to face today. By spreading this positive energy, you're enhancing the lives of the people around you. This is the most important and beautiful thing any human being can do with their life.

-Thank you for staying with me all the way through our meditation practice today.

Session #2 - For Your Child

-Hello! Welcome to this exciting new game that I'll be teaching you today. You will love it! How do I know this? Because this game is fun, inventive and very much perfect for you. I will start by thanking you for choosing this game to play today.

-Let me tell you about some of the features of this game. First, the name: the game we're about to play is called the positive meditation game. It is about how the mind makes you super-boy or super-girl, just like you'd see in comic books or superhero movies. Did you know that you can actually do that in real life? If you didn't, good news: meditation is here to make you just that, a positive superhuman who's ready to conquer the world!

-How are we going to do that? Don't worry, it isn't difficult at all. All you have to do is to just relax, follow my simple instructions for a few moments and, before you know it, you'll be stronger, more relaxed and much more positive. You will be ready to tackle even the more challenging parts of your day, ready to turn those everyday tasks like homework, brushing your teeth or tidying after you play much more enjoyable.

-Are you ready to play the positive meditation game? Alright, here we go!

-The first thing that I want you to do right now is to simply find a very comfortable place where you can sit for a little while. I'll be honest, the game takes more than a few minutes. But then again this is normal, as you can't master the art of positive meditation in just a few seconds!

-As you get comfortable in your chair, on the sofa or even on your bed, heck, some people even sit on the floor, I want you to focus your attention on our positive meditation tool today: your breathing. The breathing will be our tool for the practice. Every time something goes wrong, we will get back to the breathing. Every time our focus gets out of order, we will be focusing on the breath. It's that simple.

-When was the last time you focused on nothing but your breath? Some people have done it in the past. Some have briefly discovered it and saw it for what an awesome tool it is for the mind and body. But unfortunately, most people have never taken one single breath with a fully focused attention on it.

-This is what I want you to do before anything else. I want you to become best friends with your breath. I want you to become one with the simple, life-giving act of breathing.

-Relax your shoulders, your arms, your chest, your hips, your legs and your feet. Relax your neck and your head and the mind inside it. Once the entire body is tingling with calmness and relaxation, what I want you to do is to take a few deep breaths in through your nose and then out through your mouth.

-Don't make them to be just another few breaths now. I want them to be loud, serious, remarkable breaths. I want you to keep them considerate, but I also want them to be heard. If someone were to be in the room with you, I want them to hear you breathing your best breaths. Whoa, that was a tongue twister for sure!

-Continue to take a few more deep breaths, breathing in through the nose, and then exhaling out through the mouth, as you continue to feel the body getting more relaxed with each breath that you're taking.

-You are doing absolutely great!

-And with this next exhale, I want you to simply close the eyes gently. As the eyes are closing down, you will let your breath naturally return to its normal rhythm. It could mean you're going to breathe in and out through the nose for the rest of this practice, or it could mean you'll be breathing in and out through the mouth, or a combination of both. Regardless of what's in store for your breathing mode today, it is important for the breath to happen normally, naturally.

-Now that the breath has come back to its normal state, while still keeping a soft focus on it, I want you to also focus on your mind and body right now, as we begin the game of positive meditation.

-We'll start with considering how the mind is doing at this moment. If there's any thinking in the mind, all you have to do is playfully let those thoughts come and go. That's all you have to do. I know, it's not that hard to get positive superpowers, isn't it?

-Whatever the mind is thinking right now, simply notice the thoughts and then let them go. It is often that the mind thinks not only good things but also not so good things. This is completely normal. The mind works just as the other parts of your amazing body do, so it is normal to have its good and bad moments. If we get a cold and our nose is runny, we don't say the nose is bad, right? It is just the nose and it will go back to normal if we treat it well.

-It so happens to the mind as well. If we treat the mind well, by giving it complete freedom and observing over it in good and bad times, the mind will naturally calm down and focus on the positive things. All I want you to do now is to focus on the calmness of the mind. Observing the mind quietly, without any interference.

-Amazing, you are doing great!

-We will now focus on how the entire body feels. And just as we did with the mind, we will use the positive meditation or meditative state to focus on just accepting the way the body feels. You might be achy in some parts from that last ball practice. You might have some discomfort in the legs or arms from jumping on the trampoline. Your head might hurt from all of the classes you've been to today. I don't blame you! And you shouldn't blame your body either.

-Use your superpower of seeing the positive in everything and see the good in the way your body feels. If it feels awesome, then great, simply focus on observing that. And if it doesn't, also great, as you'll feel just how great it is to have a body that can take it all. To have a body that functions properly, that lets you play around all day and is home to your mind and heart and everything else in there. We'll leave the details for future biology classes.

-What an amazing thing to have, this body!

-Remember to keep that gentle focus on your breathing as you inhale and exhale through the nose or mouth. Always go back to your meditation tool whenever there's too much going on in the mind. Focusing on breathing will get you back on track from wherever you've left on.

-Very well done thus far! Now, we will be moving on to the second part of this practice, which will be us focusing on the positive aspects of your day today. Both those that have happened, and those that are about to happen later, after you're done with this practice.

-I want you to take this day step by step and focus on one aspect that was positive for each important moment of it. Let's start with waking up this morning. I know waking up early in the morning might not be the greatest thing in the world. Especially on a school day, if that's the case. But I also know there are a million reasons why waking up is still great!

-For example, it might be the delicious breakfast you've had this morning. Or maybe you've got some quality time to spend with your family, or play some games, or hang out with your pet. Just focus on that positive aspect of waking up this morning for a few moments now.

-Next, I want you to focus on the positive aspects of school or kindergarten today. There are always some great things about school that we often forget about. It's easy to focus on the negative, like the long classes, short breaks, bad lunches, crowded busses and cranky teachers. But the line between the negative and the positive is so thin, it's a shame most of us never cross it to see the good in the bad.

-For example, you might want to focus on the actual class when you're in one rather than how long or boring it is. Maybe the subject of the class is so interesting, you will find a new hobby you'll enjoy for the rest of your life. Or maybe you want to use those short breaks to make new friends, listen to people, interact with them. Speak to that one kid who wanted to talk to you and make his or her day so much better. Simply focus on a few more positive aspects of school for a few moments now.

-Remember to always pay that subtle attention to the breathing, the meditation stone for this practice.

-If it's the afternoon when you're doing this practice, I want you to focus on the positive aspects of lunch and your arrival at home after classes. What were the best moments of the day for you today? Maybe the food you've had at lunch? Maybe a great talk you've had with a girl or a boy you like? Maybe seeing your parents or relatives at home after a long day at school? Whatever the reasons might be, focus on the positive things of the day today.

-I also want you to now focus on the positive aspects of the day from now until bedtime. I want you to visualize what you're about to do today and pick those aspects that are the best, the most amazing, the moments you're waiting for with all of your heart and soul.

-It might happen that you're about to go to a birthday party later. Or maybe you're going to the movies with your parents. Also, you might just be sitting at home and enjoying a few games with your family or even by yourself. Whatever it is, I want you to focus on this positivity that you'll keep with you for the rest of the day today.

-Also, I want you to visualize how you're going to stay positive throughout the day today even if things don't turn out the way you planned them to. If the party gets cancelled, I want you to be thankful for being invited and for having all of the past parties you enjoyed and on which you can reflect.

-If there are no more tickets to the movies, I want you to be grateful for the movie running tomorrow or the day after and you being able to go see it then. If you feel that you haven't done so good at one of your favorite games today, I want you to reflect on what you can learn from this experience and what are you taking with you that will make your playing experience so much better next time!

-Positivity, this is all that you have to remember all through the day today. That's it, that is your new superpower, being positive, staying positive, playing positive. Everything is so much better if you keep a positive attitude towards it.

-Awesome job, I am so proud of how you're feeling right now. And you should be, too!

-Let's now move to the next part of this meditation today, which is pretty simple: all you have to do is to listen to a couple of affirmations. These are not just phrases that are meant to make you a tad more positive today. You already are a great, positive, joyful being. These are meant to get behind you whenever you feel like that positivity inside you is for any reason fading out.

-We will focus on listening to these affirmations and then talk about each and every one of them for a moment, before moving to the next one. In total, we will listen to ten of these affirmations today, taking them one by one and gently focus on the breath while doing so.

-Alright, we'll begin right away!

-Let's start the practice of affirmations with the first one. All you have to do is to listen to it, while completely focusing on the words and being aware of your breath. We will repeat each affirmation twice. It's that simple. Here we go with the first one right now.

-The more I like myself, the more others will like me. I am becoming better with each day because of my positive attitude.

-The more I like myself, the more others will like me. I am becoming better with each day because of my positive attitude.

<<PAUSE FOR 5 SECONDS>>

-Good. Liking oneself is the first step towards being able to adopt a positive attitude. By loving yourself a little more each day, you become a better version of yourself and are also able to adopt a positive attitude much easier.

-Here we go for the second affirmation of this practice today. Remember to breathe and concentrate your full attention on the words you're about to hear. Let's listen carefully.

-I am happy to be here for me and my friends. I have people who care about me and will help me if I need.

-I am happy to be here for me and my friends. I have people who care about me and will help me if I need.

<<PAUSE FOR 5 SECONDS>>

-Being grateful for your friends and happy to be here not just for you, but for them as well is a sign of maturity and compassion. Having those people you can count on and care for is crucial for the development of ideologies that will help you tremendously in life later. You'll become a better and better human being just by simply caring for your friend, relative, parents or grandparents, teachers and colleagues.

-Next comes the third meditation of this series. We will once again focus our attention on the breath, while keeping a close attention to the words. It will help you better incorporate the information into your deep mind.

-I am always learning more about who I am and what matters to me. I am developing my own mind and body by doing so.

-I am always learning more about who I am and what matters to me. I am developing my own mind and body by doing so.

<<PAUSE FOR 5 SECONDS>>

-Good one! Learning is not something you do just in school, right? It's a universal, life-long process. You are learning something right now, just by doing this practice. You are learning when you wake up, go to sleep, even in your dreams. By discovering more and more of the world, you're actually discovering more and more of your own self.

-Let's now take a moment to focus on the breath while we get ready for the fourth affirmation of this practice. Remember to take it in slowly and listen to it with all of your awareness. Make it so that you're not only listening with the ears, but also with the entire body and mind.

-I understand that my actions become habits so I will try to do the right thing. With each action comes an equal, opposite reaction.

-I understand that my actions become habits so I will try to do the right thing. With each action comes an equal, opposite reaction.

<<PAUSE FOR 5 SECONDS>>

-Great one this one! Every single thing that you do has a reaction in the Universe and surely, in your life. For each action that you partake, there's an equal reaction happening. It's a law of life. Making sure all of your actions are positive, and being aware they will eventually turn into habits, is crucial to having a positive, joyful, impactful life.

-We have one more affirmation to go through before we'll take a little mental break and regroup. Here's the fifth affirmation for you. Listen to it carefully while gently focusing on the breath as well.

-I am an intelligent being, but I don't know everything. While I keep myself open to new things, I am able to keep myself growing.

-I am an intelligent being, but I don't know everything. While I keep myself open to new things, I am able to keep myself growing.

<<PAUSE FOR 5 SECONDS>>

-Nice one! Intelligence does not mean just reading about things and memorizing. Intelligence, the ultimate type of intelligence, is understanding that there is something to learn from each and every situation that happens to us. Staying open minded about everything is key.

-It is now time to take a small break from the practice of affirmations. We will be gently regrouping. It's now time to stretch for a short while. You may do this with your eyes closed or open, but remember to do this gently, not all of a sudden. Relax your hands, your legs and your body. Let go of any tension in the neck or back. Regain some motion by slowly moving your muscles around without actually leaving your spot.

-And then gently refocus your attention on your pose. Staying calm once again in the same posture, whether it's on the floor, or on a chair.

Close your eyes once more if you've decided to open them. If you didn't, simply sit back the way you were as we're getting ready to resume on the affirmations. Once again, take a few breaths in and out through the nose.

-We are now ready to listen to the sixth affirmation of our practice today. As you did until now, please take a moment to focus on the breath and then listen carefully,

-I love myself and my community. I am proud to represent the values that matter to me and my family.

-I love myself and my community. I am proud to represent the values that matter to me and my family.

<<PAUSE FOR 5 SECONDS>>

-Awesome! Remember the last time you needed help? Remember when you asked for help and then one of your friends or neighbors, family or people around you jumped and helped you? This is what it means to love the community in which you live as well as yourself in equal matters. Being yourself while being a part of a community is a great way to live and spread equality and joy throughout your surroundings.

-Here we go now for the seventh affirmation of the day today. Once again, remember to keep your focus on the words you're about to hear, while gently becoming aware of the breath.

-I am responsible for my own happiness. I am the only one to decide how to approach every situation I encounter and if and how to make the best of it.

-I am responsible for my own happiness. I am the only one to decide how to approach every situation I encounter and if and how to make the best of it.

<<PAUSE FOR 5 SECONDS>>

-Your parents, family and friends can help you in many ways. They can try to make you feel happy when you are sad, they can try to make you feel brave when you are scared, they can try to make you feel confident when you are not sure. But they cannot make you feel one way or another, they cannot decide for you your thoughts and feelings. You are the only one who can decide that. Which is great! Why? Because you never depend on external things to make you feel happy or brave or confident. It is all inside you already and you only need to choose to feel it.

-Very good. You are doing great so far and we are so close to the end of this practice, by the way. Just a little more patience from you and you'll be done.

-We are now preparing for affirmation number eight for the day. Calmly bring the awareness back to the breathing. Here we go with the powerful quote, so listen carefully.

-I always learn from everything that happens, even when I don't like it. I know that everything will pass and I can learn and grow from every experience that happens to me.

-I always learn from everything that happens, even when I don't like it. I know that everything will pass and I can learn and grow from every experience that happens to me.

<<PAUSE FOR 5 SECONDS>>

-Alright, good one. We don't always like the way a certain situation makes us feel. Maybe we quarreled with a friend over a game, maybe our favorite toy broke, maybe our mom or dad did not allow us to do something we really wanted to do. It is absolutely fine and natural to feel upset at that moment. Let yourself feel it. And after a few moments, try to gather yourself and think about what you can learn from what just happened. What you can learn about what is important to your friend, what you can learn about how to care for your toys, what you can learn about your mom or dad's feelings and what they tried to protect you from. We can always learn from anything that happens and become more empowered from it.

-As we're moving along we've now reached affirmation number nine. For this one, we'll also be focusing on the breathing while keeping a gentle eye on the words that you're about to hear.

-Other people's opinions are not the reality. It is only their reality. I create my own reality in which I am a wonderful human being.

-Other people's opinions are not the reality. It is only their reality. I create my own reality in which I am a wonderful human being.

<<PAUSE FOR 5 SECONDS>>

-Fantastic one! Good people will reflect their kindness and compassion, and you'll feel their goodness, even without any words.

As we're closing in with the affirmations practice today, let's give it one more effort and listen to the last, tenth one. Breathe gently and focus your mind and body into listening to this last one.

-I am completely unique and therefore, there are no rules to what I am and am not.

-I am completely unique and therefore, there are no rules to what I am and am not.

<<PAUSE FOR 5 SECONDS>>

-Very well! Once you say about someone or about yourself that you are this and that, you are closing in on the many different opportunities of becoming something more than you are right now. You are closing in on your own self, on your own life and goals. You are restricting your ways. If you have no rules, mental rules, in place about who you are or who you are not, you are letting yourself be, become, grow and evolve into your ultimate self.

-Now that you've attained this new positive superpower, it is time to get back to the present moment and end this meditation practice. We will do this gently, not in just one sweep. Gradually, we will leave the practice behind but also stay aware of its immense benefits. We're going to be coming back to the breathing, the ultimate source of life within all of us.

-While focusing on the breath, please feel free to regain control of the body.

-Feel the way the body feels on the floor or on the chair, the weight of the arms, legs, chest, head and neck. Feel the points of contact on these surfaces, even on where the skin touches the clothes on your body. When this happens, simply notice it and do not think about it for too long.

-Listen to the many sounds around you that you've naturally blocked until now. Smell the scents you can smell around you. Become more and more aware of the different things that you can sense around you without opening your eyes. See if you can spot any sounds from cars or planes outside your house. Any smells coming from a beautiful flower, or any tastes that you might have tasted earlier in the day.

-And gently now, without making any fast movements, open your eyes and fully emerge from the meditative state into a fully conscious come back into the conscious world.

-As you go about your day today, remember this practice. Remember the body scan. Remember the affirmations, what they mean and how they've helped you see beyond your simple nature that you've known this far in life. Remember to keep a positive attitude in your life, regardless of what you're doing today, tomorrow or anytime soon. Be kind and gentle to everything and everyone, especially to yourself.

-Thank you for being a part of this practice. Looking forward to meeting you here again.

Before we part, I would like to once again remind you that as a self-publishing author, reviews are the lifeblood of my work. I would be very happy and thankful if you could take a few moments to leave a review on Amazon. I truly appreciate your time.

REFERENCES

Bailey, B. (2019, August 8). The Three Types of Consequences and How to Give Them. Retrieved from https://consciousdiscipline.com/three-types-of-consequences/.

Nelsen, J. (2019, May 19). Kind and Firm Parenting. Retrieved from https://www.positivediscipline.com/articles/kind-and-firm-parenting.

Nelsen, J. (2019, June 23). Limited Choices. Retrieved from https://www.positivediscipline.com/articles/limited-choices.

Nelsen, J. (2007). *Positive discipline A-Z: 1001 solutions to everyday parenting problems.* New York: Three Rivers Press. Retrieved from https://www.pdfdrive.com/positive-discipline-a-z-a-1001-solutions-to-everyday-parenting-problems-e195032860.html

Printed in Great Britain
by Amazon

61219202R00092